Mental Models:

Learn How to Improve Decision Making, Problem Solving, Develop Better Strategic Thinking and Reasoning Ability to Avoid Cognitive Biases

Joe Silva

Table of Contents

Introduction

There are plenty of books on this subject on the market, thanks again for choosing this one! Every effort was made to ensure it is full of as much useful information as possible, and please enjoy!

What Is A Mental Model? All You Need To Know About Mental Models

Mental models are nothing but thought processes through which a human being tries to explain to himself and to others, how the real world works. It is a kind of inner symbol of representation of external reality, hypothetical, which plays an important role in cognition - that is, in the way we apprehend the world. It is the mental models of each of us that define how we perceive what happens around us, how each event will affect us, how we will think, and how we will act. Each person has their own mental model, which is the result of all their experiences, life history, and situations.

In short, the mental model can be described as a broad view of the world, acquired through past experiences. They are presuppositions, generalizations, or even deep-rooted images that influence the way we see the world and act. These thoughts help us look at the world from a different perspective than others, and it also helps us understand the right from wrong. It is said that no two perspectives or thoughts are the same that is because of the mental model of each individual. This book will help you understand what the mental model is all about.

What Does This Have To Do With Management?

All because we are talking about the world view of managers. There is a lot of talk today about the business model, but that is only a part of the equation. The main model in question is the mental one, for there are several studies that prove that the mental model of leaders can be responsible for the success - or failure - of a company.

There are seven basic dimensions that can drive entrepreneurs' mental models to perform their organizations better. They are knowledge, emotional ability, linear mental capacity, relationship, mission and strategy, creativity, and vocation.

The Example of Southwest Airlines

According to an article from the Harvard Business Review, the US airline industry is emblematic of what can happen when companies reshape the business model without changing the mental model.

For more than 40 years, the Southwest Airlines Company has been breaking models in the airline industry there. Already 43 years of profitability - an absolute record for the segment. The model is simple: while traditional companies such as United and Delta operate with multiclass cabs, heterogeneous fleets, and flights by connections, Southwest focuses on reduced rates, with only one-class cabins, homogeneous fleets, and no-connection routes.

At first, many companies tried to copy this model. But why did not it work? Because, from the outset, the mental model of Southwest Airlines co-founder Herb Kelleher was well-defined: as competitors, he saw not only airlines, but cars, buses, and trains.

Kelleher's idea was to make air travel possible to anyone who had not been able to do so before. Thus, the mental model was not focused on how to gain market share from other companies, but on creating a brand new market for the airline industry.

"It is incidental that we operate with airplanes."

The differences between their mental models do not stop there. The following statement by Herb Kelleher is well-known: "I tell my employees that we are in the service business and that it is incidental that we operate with airplanes." That is, according to this view of the world, Southwest serves people using airplanes, while other airlines fly airplanes to carry people. Did you notice the difference?

Because of this, the efforts of large companies to replicate the model failed. Continental Lite, United's Ted, and Delta's Song: none of them took off, and managers blamed the poor execution. When Continental ended Lite's operations, CEO Gordon Bethune said the initiative "was not implemented in an orchestrated way." But the real reason for the failure was the fact that the new business model was deployed without an equivalent mental model behind it.

Traditional airlines are still thinking about their business from airplanes instead of serving people. The mental model is still to capture market slices instead of expanding that market, and the measure of success remains based on how successful the aircraft uses and experiences on board.

What does all this teach us? That copying a business model without a mental model that supports it will certainly lead to very frustrating results. You need to change the way you think before you change what you do - and then change what you measure to close the cycle.

According to the same Harvard Business Review article, you should have, as an example of what not to do, the recent pronouncement of Volkswagen, in which the company has said it plans to outperform Tesla in the race for electric vehicles. The promise of VW is that the brand will make huge leaps with a modular car assembly platform.

The problem is that in this case too, a large company is replicating a business model using the wrong mental model. Volkswagen is an automaker that uses technology, while Tesla, on the other hand, knows it's a technology company that rides cars. And this, as we have seen, makes all the difference.

So, now you know: before you reshape your business model, stop and reflect on your mental model. It is he who will legitimize change - and produce the results you are sure to seek.

Chapter 1 - Mental Models: What They Are, Sources and Impacts on Behavior

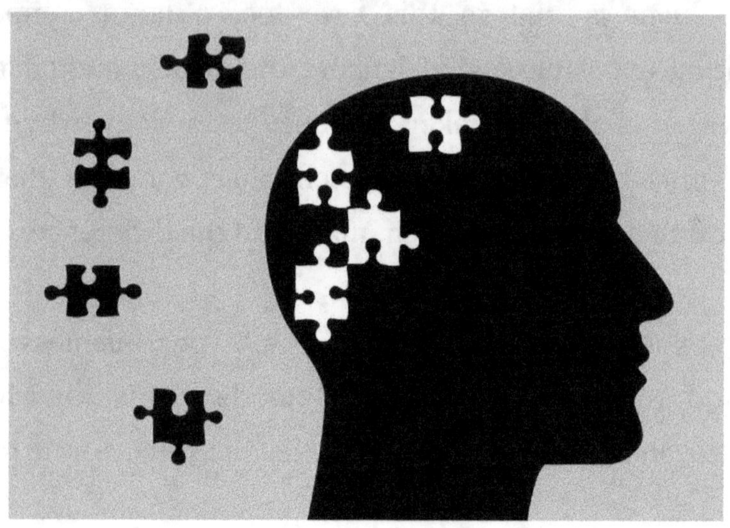

"No one is equal to anyone." "We all think different." "The unanimity is dumb."

You may have heard some of these statements at least once in your life, but you may not know they have everything to do with so-called mental models. But how do these constructions happen? Where do our thoughts come from? Why do we make certain decisions and not others? Why are certain behaviors seen as obvious by us?

If these questions leave you curious, then this is the right book for you. Keep reading on. In addition to explaining the concept of mental models, let's talk about their impact on our routine.

Just reiterating the most important question before we talk about anything else:

What Are Mental Models?

We can describe mental models as the way people interpret everything they see around them. That is why there are different views on the same fact. This means that, based on their experiences and other elements - which we will see below -, the human being analyzes each event and defines how it will act in a given situation.

For the researcher and writer Daniel Goleman, the father of emotional intelligence, the definition of mental models is quite clear. According to him, the term refers to the way people organize their eyes and thoughts, perceive and behave before the world, in such a way that the experiences they live have some meaning for themselves.

The big challenge is to open the mind and try to change these pre-designed models a little bit. The ability to try to put yourself in the other person's place, the so-called empathy, is an interesting exercise to observe reality from a prism different than yours.

Finding that your mental pattern is the only possible one or is somehow, more important than others', is also something that needs to be worked on to avoid unnecessary conflicts and disagreements. Okay, let me ask you this next: Have you ever stopped to think about your mental models and how much you can shape them? What are the sources from which we derive our mental models?

The mental models of each are created, basically, from four main sources: the nervous system, language, culture, and personal history. Check below to see how each of them gets constructed.

Nervous System

Also known as a biological filter, it concerns certain limitations, as well as the physiological and cognitive capacities that each human being has. For example, a person who is color-blind will not have the same interpretation of one picture as another who can recognize all the colors of the landscape. Similarly, comparing human characteristics with that of some animals would also be unequal to us and would offer different experiences for both sides.

While the man's ear has a limit of vibrations to be heard per minute, something close to 20,000 Hertz, dogs can perceive sounds much sharper than that. The human night vision also does not compare with that of a bat or even a cat. Our visual range is infinitely inferior to that of an eagle. It impacts on how these living beings act. A shrill whistle may be hurting your dog's hearing aid while you may be hearing almost nothing.

Language

The second filter through which our mental models pass is that of language. Around the world, this phenomenon is very evident. How many objects and foods are the same, but are given a different denomination depending on the region in which you are?

Tangerine, bergamot, gossip, or mimosa? Pipe, pandorga, or parrot? Cassava, casava, or cazzava? Certainly, you have heard some of these terms, perhaps others have never heard of. But each of these words has the same meaning, and what varies is the region in which they are used. The accents and characteristic expressions of each part of the world is also something to be highlighted.

Language has to do with two people seeing the same thing and understanding it differently. Numbers, which are also a form of communication, as words, for example, may have varying meanings and interpretations for different types of professionals. When looking at a company's billing, the treasurer or accountant has a distinct view of the engineer. Not that a construction project specialist cannot read the numbers presented here, but he is not prepared to make the distinctions that the financial experts know of and are ready to make.

Now the engineer has the command of language to read complex equations and calculations, linked to structural questions. A knowledge that the accountant or the treasurer does not possess. What we are trying to say is that all these experts are certainly able to see the numbers and read the materials, but only a few of them are able to master the language and correctly interpret what is written. This, of course, is according to their expertise.

Personal History

We all have a past and carry information over the years. This baggage, in one way or another, interferes with our mental models more or less directly, depending on the case. Elements such as race, sexual orientation, family history, economic situation, educational background, relationship with parents and teachers, among other variables, affect our decisions.

Some behaviors that may seem obvious, logical, and natural to you, they may be viewed as misplaced and purposeless to others, and there's nothing wrong with that. This is because creation and past and assimilated values are different from person to person. Even at the beginning of our childhood, when we do not yet have even a critical capacity for reflection, information is incorporated into our way of being. The examples of this filter of mental models are innumerable.

Imagine a sports event that has as commentator a former athlete of the sport and a specialized journalist who studied the whole theoretical part of the game. The opinions will be different, since the former athlete tends to go to the practical side, based on his personal experience, to have acted in the function. He will bring cases of the profession, situations experienced by him. On the other hand, the journalist will weigh for the technical part and in the information that he studied and analyzed as someone who evaluates the sport in a critical way. And this does not only happen in the professional field but also in the personal one.

How many people do not deprive themselves of certain experiences because they have had a bad history in some specific situation? The important thing is to understand that this filter deals with personal history. That is, the present and the future will be impacted by these trials of the past. It is up to each person to best deal with their traumas and their memories so as not to fall into an infinite looping cycle that prevents them from moving forward.

Culture

In a way, it is very similar to the previous source of mental models. The difference is that this kind of thinking pattern, let's call it that, is influenced by the collective imagination and not by the individual one. That is, your way of seeing the reality around you is impacted by the culture to which you were subjected or submitted to throughout your life. And do not fall into that mistake of believing that your culture is superior to the other. Something like that does not exist.

Western civilizations have different customs from the eastern people, for example, but that does not mean that one is better than the other. For example, some Arab Muslim countries claim that a man can marry more than one wife. However, around the world, polygamy is not accepted. Can you disagree with the way other people view this issue of marriage? Of course, you can. Your customs and personal experience will cause you to question these values. What is wrong is to have prejudice with a tradition that is not yours, and you certainly do not completely understand.

Because it is the only filter of collective mental models, culture can be viewed in two distinct ways. If, on one hand, it is positive because it helps to maintain order and structure a way of thinking that extends to a large number of people, on the other, it tends to be limiting and conservative. Mostly, for this reason, cultural, mental models are the most difficult to transform and adapt to new realities.

Chapter 2 - The Origin of Mental Models

As we have seen, our mental models emerge long before we are born. Culturally speaking, its origin points to hundreds or even thousands of years before us. But over time, our biological limitations, our personal history, and our appropriation by the different types of language will guide the way we think and act. It is from this combination of factors that we build and firm opinions. More important than knowing the origin of these mental models, is trying to take the reins on them. Not to be carried away by the automatism of preconceived concepts is the main challenge of the routine. After all, it's not because you've always understood a subject in a certain way that needs to go on like this.

Mental Models That Block Creativity

"I cannot do it." "I do not have the capacity." "I will not try because it will not work."

These are typical phrases that we repeat in difficult situations that require going beyond the ordinary. But maybe it's time you re-thought the use of each phrase and line you speak. The human unconscious sometimes imposes barriers on our actions. These are the so-called limiting thoughts, which make us fear new and different experiences. It is that kind of reasoning that only leads to the commonplace and prevents something creative from being externalized. Do you know those traditional phrases, the clichés like "every politician is a thief" or "blonde is dumb"?

The point here is to leave such expressions aside and allow yourself to go further, to understand the meaning behind each story and not just repeat what most propagates as truth.

Discover your Mental Models

You may know the origin of your mental models, but have you stopped to wonder why they affect you in a certain way? Trying to find out, in fact, what these patterns are and to understand what they mean is a way to appropriate even more of your thoughts and emotions.

Want to understand how? Check out the following tips which I have collated and listed below:

Self

The first question you should ask yourself is: do I really know myself?

Looking at yourself and seeking answers is the first step in understanding how you relate to people and the world. Aggression, for example, is a fairly common feeling among those who try only to stifle the struggles they daily struggle within to find out what they expect from life.

Empathy

As you begin to practice self-knowledge and understand your own doubts, it will become much easier to relate to the outside world. This also means exercising empathy. The simple exercise of putting oneself in the other's place opens up a universe of infinite possibilities of understanding. You will see that your colleague's attitude was based on his four sources and filters, which may be completely different from yours.

Respect

After all, the natural way is that of respect for contrary opinions. But this is also an exercise you must bring about. Each individual has his/her own mental model, created from their personal, cultural, and other experiences - and there is nothing wrong with it. The important thing is not to make it the only option.

By performing these activities, you will be much closer to discovering and controlling your own thought patterns. Now, I am guessing that the following question will be the logically next query on your mind:

How to Make Use of Knowledge?

In order for our models not to close in on themselves, we must always be in search of knowledge. It's not because something worked 20 years ago, so it will always be the best alternative. This means our mental models need to be expanded.

Do you know that child's toy in which each geometrical figure should be placed in the space corresponding to its design? Our mental models work in a similar way. And no, I am not joking.

Your experience only gave you the reading of a circle. However, the moment offers you a square. The easiest may seem to cut the edges of the square so that it serves in the space of the sphere, but a person who adapts and seeks knowledge will try to understand the reading of the figure and what lies behind it.

Mental models are all about management. It is not difficult to look back and remember big brands that have failed or lost their market space. Accustomed to a different world, they were not able to adapt to cultural and technological changes.

That is, based on their own mental models, the managers did not understand that the transformation was a basic condition for the company to continue occupying its space. And startups quickly occupied these gaps, which were waiting to be filled. It is something that cannot be ignored.

The Influence of Mental Models on Corporate Results

The success story of Southwest Airlines, a Texan airline, shows what we have just said. The company, which has giant competitors such as Delta and United, is the only one in the industry to make a profit for 43 consecutive years. This is because, since its foundation, it has an open mental model that allows identifying market trends.

While the other companies are investing in state-of-the-art aircraft, with class A, B, C and D cabins and multi-stop flights, Southwest has more modest aircraft models without stipulating socioeconomic divisions for passengers and non-stop travel. This is a type of business that grew out of the perception that there was a specific consumer who had purchasing power but not enough to pay for all the luxuries of an air trip.

Looking at the service in a different way made it possible to enter a segment that had not been explored until then. Hence, you might ask, "Oh, but have not competitors tried to repeat the business model?" They tried, but they did not have the same success as we mentioned before. This happened because the public did not buy the idea and preferred to continue flying with the company that from the beginning, was dedicated to it.

How Does The Mental Model Of Leaders Impact On Company Performance?

Believe it or not, mental models of leaders do impact company performance a lot. Any and every decision made by a company's leaders is in some way based on their mental models. That is, the impact is direct and appears in each of the choices made.

Mental Models in Leadership

Want a positive example of a mental model of a good leader? He is the one who takes responsibility and does not blame anyone. This type of manager is proactive and shares his accomplishments with the team. When he realizes that something is wrong, he tries to find a solution, instead of just pointing out the problem. It is someone who helps resolve conflicts and seeks to hear what others have to say. If you want to follow the model of a good leader, that is the way.

Brief Conclusion

Mental models are present throughout our lives, and they start existing since even before we were born. As much as you might try to ignore them, they will appear in your decisions. They are so natural that we often do not even notice it.

The important thing is to know how to use them in our favor, in a way that impacts our actions positively. To get there, do not forget these three words: self-knowledge, empathy, and respect.

Understanding the mental models that are part of your life is fundamental to understanding human behavior as well. In fact, mental models can determine a person's success or failure. I have long wanted to write a book or something else about mental models, as much as I like the subject. When I ask anyone I talk to on the topic or even otherwise as to what this means, some people look at me apprehensively and are waiting for a tip, but the question is mine, and I always try to extract the answer according to the general knowledge of the group. When you understand the concept and seek to associate it in practice, the journey becomes less painful.

Understanding the basis of human behavior and the keys to personal fulfillment depends on understanding the meaning and importance of mental models in your life. Whether you know it or not, mental models define your ability to act and react to the simplest things and the hardest things in life; that is, they define your behavior.

First, it is necessary to know the sources of mental models and the way they are formed. According to Daniel Goleman, author of the bestselling book called Emotional Intelligence, the sources of mental models are the way humans organize and give meaning to their experiences. According to Goleman, human behavior is conditioned by mental models, and these, in turn, are defined based on four assumptions:

Biology: labeling the human being's ability to perform based on its physiological limitations. Does the fact that someone is tall or short, black or white, hairy or bald, fat or thin, beautiful or less favored in terms of beauty, should be a factor of inclusion or exclusion in the job market? For many companies, this is how it works, unfortunately. Have you ever read a job advertisement in the newspaper with the following words: Do you need a Chubby Secretary, short, and everything which more or less means something about the appearance and less about the skills or intelligence?

Language: is the medium in which the consciousness of the human being is structured. When you hear a Northeasterner, a Santa Catarina, a gaucho from the pampas, a Paulista from the interior or a carioca with a conversation with that typical accent of his region, what comes to your mind? Do not say you've never labeled someone because of your accent? Enjoy! But baaah !!!

Culture: within any group - families, industries, organizations, and nations - collective mental models develop from shared experiences. Thus culture can be considered a collective mental model. If you are the child of Jew, Italian, Greek, German, or Japanese, it does not matter, and there is a set of values or assumptions typical of each culture. Somehow this affects relationships, hence the difficulties of admitting in some cultures the union of people from different roots.

Personal experience: concerns race, gender, nationality, ethnic origin, social and economic condition, family influences, level of education, how we were treated by our parents, siblings, teachers and childhood partners. The way we begin to work and achieve self-sufficiency is also the fruit of our personal experience, and that is key to our success.

Because of all this, some phrases become common in your daily life and when you least expect it, inadvertently slip, without the least concern for the reflection of your words. What counts for one country or culture is not necessarily valid for another. Have you ever uttered any of these phrases?

All men are equal! It means that your father and that person you both admire are also. You cannot trust women! Even your mother, your wife, and your sisters?

All politicians are equal! Including that his relative who had been very hard-fought and found a job for his entire family that was in trouble?

The little with God is enough! Believe me, if this is true, the most you will achieve is definitely that 'little,' and at the same time, you will continue to envy the rich for the rest of your life.

This is not going to work, and it has always been like this here! This is one of the most well-known mental models in organizations that are doomed to fail.

I'm poor, but I'm happy! Do you know some poor, in the literal sense of the word, happy?

The important thing is to win! More important than winning is contributing and not being overwhelmed by defeat. If the world were made only of victors, learning would not exist.

These are some of the thousands of mental models established based on our biology, language, culture, and personal experience. When taken literally, mental models are capable of causing real havoc in our personal and professional lives. However, you should not ignore them, just be careful to avoid prejudices designed solely on the basis of values that may be part of one culture and not another.

For FredyKofman, author of Metamanagement, the mental model is the set of meanings, assumptions, rules of reasoning, inferences, and so on, which leads us to make a certain interpretation. They define how we perceive, feel, think, and interact. Therefore, it is fundamental to immerse ourselves in different cultures, disciplines, experiences, and languages without losing our origins.

All cultures have something to teach about human behavior from different angles of vision; just know how to respect them. The Jewish maxim expressed in the Talmud helps us better understand this reasoning: "We do not see things as they are, we see things as we are." Think about it and be happy!

Chapter 3 - Individual And Collective Mental Models: Beware, Automatic Routines Are Inflexible!

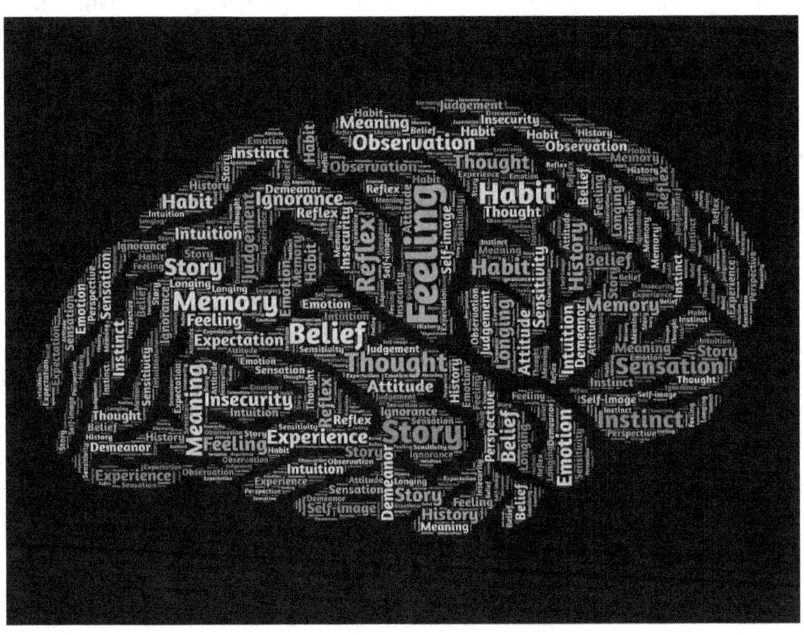

The mental model is the set of meanings, assumptions, rules of reasoning, inferences, etc, which leads us to make a certain interpretation. As Peter Senge puts it, "they are deeply rooted assumptions, generalizations, illustrations, images or stories that influence our way of understanding and acting on the world." They work permanently subconsciously, in our personal life, in the professional sphere in our social organizations, helping us give meaning to reality and operate effectively. Mental models condition all our interpretations and actions. They define how we perceive, feel, think, and interact.

Different mental models can motivate different perceptions, feelings, opinions, and actions. For example, for the accountant, a certain result of a company is showing stability, and that should keep its course. For the vice president of marketing, the result proves that the company is stagnant and should start a new advertising campaign. For a board member, it's the "disapproval" of CEO policy. To an investor, it suggests that it is time to sell your shares; for another, it is time to buy. The result is the same; the worldly context is the same; what explains the differences are the different mental models.

Different perceptions, opinions, and actions are not a problem in themselves. They become conflicting, in fact, when each person believes that their way of seeing things (according to their mental model) is the only way of seeing them; at least the only "reasonable." Of course, the idea of "rationality" is an opinion conditioned by the mental model of each person. Everyone believes that their model is the valid model. Instead of using different perceptions to expand their perspectives and integrate them into a common vision, each of the interlocutors clings to their own point of view. Rather than probing the other's reasoning to understand his mental model, the interlocutors wage a battle to determine who is right, who has the "right" interpretation of reality.

Mental models are also the file that contains routine behaviors. As we have seen, in initiating a practice (such as driving a car, for example), one has to pay conscious attention to making unscheduled decisions. But as time passes, it develops the capacity to act automatically, transferring those decisions to the unconscious and taking advantage of what Gregory Bateson calls "the habit economy." This economy is fundamental to life since, without it, it would be impossible to act with the speed required by circumstances. But it also has a cost: automatic routines are inflexible.

The inflexibility of habit is crucial to operating efficiently in stable contexts. Like the autopilot of an airplane, the habit allows the human pilot to pay attention to other things. But flying with autopilot in the middle of a storm is very dangerous. Lack of flexibility and adaptation to changes in context is one of the main causes of species extinction (such as dinosaurs), crops (such as Roman), companies (99 out of 100 disappear without their first 10 years, and the estimated average of life of Fortune 500 companies is less than 40 years), families (60% of marriages in the world end in divorce) and people (according to recent data, 50% of deaths before age 40 can be attributed to people's behavior).

The filters through which we human beings organize and give meaning to our experiences come from four sources: biology, language, culture, and personal history. These four sources also determine the "usual" response to certain circumstances, programmed in the mental model. Just to throw some more light on the sources we had mentioned briefly before, I will try explaining them a bit further in the following paragraphs:

Biology

The first filter of mental models is the nervous system. We have physiological limitations that prevent us from perceiving certain phenomena with our senses. The reach of the human ear, for example, is 20 to 20,000 vibrations per second, while the dogs can hear shades higher and the elephants, more serious tones. The night vision of the human does not compare with that of the feline, and our vision at a distance is far inferior to that of the hawk. In terms of longitude from where the human being is able to directly see the frequencies that are between 380 and 680 millimeters, that is, a tiny band of the electromagnetic spectrum.

The impossibility of perceiving implies the impossibility to act. While the dog responds to an ultrasonic whistle, the person does not even hear it. While the bat operates in utter darkness, one loses himself. That's why we, humans, invent instruments such as sonar and radar to expand the perceptual reach of our senses and, consequently, our ability to act.

Our interconnection with the world is much more complicated than we think. The objective theory of perception states that the world "out there" creates direct changes and produces effects on the nervous system "in here." Challenging this theory, Humberto Maturana and Francisco Varela argue that the outside world can only produce disturbances in the nervous system. The subject's perceptual experience is much more determined by the very structure of his nervous system than by external disturbance. In The Tree of Knowledge, Maturana and Varela define the nervous system as a closed system. This idea contradicts the traditional notion that it defines it as "an instrument that gets information from the environment and builds a representation of the world, which the body uses to calculate the behavior appropriate for its survival. According to Maturana and Varela", as far as biology and human cognitive structures are concerned, the whole world of our experiences is within ourselves; there is no such thing as the outside experience.

This theory explains why all human beings observe the same image when they look at an object, even when none of them can experience the outside world for themselves. The similarity of our biology allows us to operate in a common reality. Maturana and Varela affirm that what the person experiences is "(reality)" and not "reality." Thus written, in parentheses, "(reality)" denotes the inner experience of the field of energies, external and unknowable, which we call "reality" without parentheses. We live in an inter-subjective (reality), not because the (reality) we see is the real, objective external reality, but because the environment awakens similar responses in our nervous systems.

Language

The second filter of our mental models is language. Language is the medium in which the consciousness of the human being is structured. Language is the space of meaning in which reality appears intelligible and communicable. Thanks to language, we can communicate with ourselves and with others about what exists around us and within us.

The traditional understanding of language is "label theory." According to this theory, we see things in the world as they are and then apply a name, a label. This is the primary use of language: a descriptive system for labeling and classifying preexisting and therefore, independent perceptions. This theory is incomplete and only accounts for a very small function of language. Researchers of cognition, brain, and consciousness have concluded that language categories are not labels applied to preexisting perceptions; on the contrary, they precondition and define perception first: the person does not speak of what he sees, but only sees what he can speak of.

The accountant "watches" on a balance sheet things that the mechanical engineer does not see. Not that the engineer does not see those same numbers; he does not have the distinctions that the accountant (the language) has to interpret those numbers. The mechanical engineer can "read" a system of differential equations that is totally incomprehensible to the meter. Not that the accountant does not see those same signs; he does not have the distinctions that the engineer (the language) has to interpret those signals. The ability to make distinctions and to order the world into operational categories is what is called "intelligence."

Culture

The third source of mental models is culture. We could consider culture as a collective mental model. As Edgard Schein defines, "culture is a pattern of shared basic assumptions learned by a group during the process of solving their problems of external adaptation and internal integration. The proof that this pattern of assumptions works is that it has worked well enough to be considered valid and therefore apt to be taught to new members as the correct way to perceive, think, and feel the themes concerning the group".

"Here, the decisions are taken by consensus." "Here we buy from the supplier who has the best prices." "Here, the men go out to work while the women stay inside." "Here, the women are independent and make their own lives." "Nature is a resource to be used by man." "Nature is sacred, and man's job is to preserve it."Each of these phrases illustrates a cultural premise. Ideas coalesce into a collective mental model that organizes the (reality) of a culture.

Within any group (families, professions, organizations, industries, nations), collective mental models evolve based on shared experiences. Throughout its history, group members must face challenges. In response, they develop a habitual way (in the sense given by Bateson) of interpreting situations and taking action. This becomes a part of the collective mental model and passes from generation to generation as the "knowledge" of the group. The problem is that with its retrogression in the night of time, such knowledge loses its experiential root and becomes an absolute truth. Instead of being "the way in which our group has effectively responded to the challenges of the past," one now has "the only correct way of responding to the challenges of the present and the future."

Collective mental models are also a double-edged sword, as are individual ones: on the one hand, they help the group structure the effective and efficient realization of their reality, based on past experiences; but, on the other hand, determine the range of possible future experiences. This self-validating system helps maintain stability and meaning within a group - indeed, in times of drastic changes, culture (which is always essentially conservative) can turn into a lead lifesaver. Challenges to shared beliefs create anxiety and entrenchment. Changing cultural presuppositions is an extremely arduous process.

Personal History

The fourth force that shapes mental models is personal history: race, gender, nationality, ethnic origin, family influences, social and economic condition, level of education, the way we have been treated by our parents, siblings, the way we started working and becoming self-sufficient, etc. All of these experiences shape the mental model one uses to navigate the world. Just as collective experiences of learning become a culture, personal learning experiences lodge in the most basic strata of consciousness and create automatic predispositions to interpret and act.

There are premises of the mental model that people adopt from their earliest childhood, even before they have any capacity for critical reflection. Throughout life, these unconsciously received ideas underlie the infinity of judgments, attitudes, and behaviors that the person considers "obvious." For example, a girl grew up in a family with an absent father and, as a result, thinks that "men are not reliable to fulfill their obligations." At the same time, the boy from the same family grows up in the opinion that "men are free to do whatever they want."

We believe that our history belongs to the past, but mental models project this past into the present and the future. Like a computer, the brain has permanent access to life experiences accumulated in memory and can extrapolate them to the present and future, as a guide to interpretation and action.

This is especially dangerous when the mental model is "anchored" in an unresolved historical situation. In such cases, one can get stuck in a repetitive circuit, symbolically recreating some traumatic experience and trying to change its outcome. For example, the individual who explodes in rebellion against his boss may be regressing to childhood in an attempt to complete pending matters with his father. The sign that denotes the regression is the total unconsciousness with which the action is carried out. Back at the house, trying to explain to his wife why he was fired, he says, "I do not know what happened; when he told me to redo all the work, I lost my temper and shouted at him. "

Personal experiences, biology, language, and culture forge each particular mental model. This model leads the person to associate with certain individuals and not with others; to think in a certain way and reject another; to undertake certain actions without even considering others; to decide what is acceptable and what is not. Each person works from his / her mental model and lives naturally in "his / her" (reality). But this (reality) may not be the same as that perceived by others, whose biology, language, culture, and personal histories are different. All human beings live in the same reality but experience it subjectively in a different way. That is why not all human beings live in the same (reality), a fact that has serious consequences.

We all have a mental model by which we define who we are, how we act, and explain the world around us. There are different types of mental models, and they are capable of leading a person to failure or success.

Sometimes your way of thinking and seeing the world will stop you from accepting the new and evolving as a person and as a professional. But there are practices that allow openness of mental models to be questioned and improved in pursuit of personal growth.

Chapter 4 - Understanding Mental Models

Mental models are fundamental to understanding human behavior. Daniel Goleman, the author of the best-selling Emotional Intelligence, defines the sources of mental models as the way humans organize and give meaning to their experiences. Thus, the author establishes four basic assumptions for the construction of mental models:

Biology: labeling the human being's ability to perform based on his or her physiological limitations, such as being tall or short, black or white, hairy or bald, fat or thin, beautiful or less favored in terms of beauty. Why do these factors still include or exclude people in the labor market?

Language: is the medium in which the consciousness of the human being is structured. When you hear a Northeasterner, a Santa Catarina, a Gaucho, a Paulista or a Carioca talking with that accent typical of your region, do you label it in some way because of your accent?

Culture: within any group - families, industries, organizations, and nations - collective mental models develop from shared experiences. In this way, culture can be considered a collective mental model. Jewish, Italian, Greek, German, or Japanese; for all, there is a set of values or assumptions typical of each culture. These values affect relationships.

Personal experience: concerns race, gender, nationality, ethnic origin, social and economic condition, family influences, level of education, how we were treated by our parents, siblings, teachers and childhood partners. The way we begin to work and achieve self-sufficiency is also the fruit of our personal experience, and that is key to our success.

After analyzing these factors, you begin to realize much more about the essence and origin of human behavior, including yours. However, more than realizing, it is necessary to begin to understand.

Self-Knowledge

To begin this understanding in a democratic way, first of all, we must develop self-knowledge. Before judging the next, judge and analyze yourself. Understand, with sincerity, all the aspects that make up your personality. Why cannot you change certain patterns of thinking? Why do you have beliefs? Whence come certain doubts so deep and difficult to answer about your opinion of the world and of the people?

Empathy

Answering fundamental questions like those mentioned above, you will know more about yourself and begin to develop empathy as well. It consists in understanding that if you have all these questions and visions about the workings of the world, other people also possess, even if it is a totally contrary form to yours. But it is a form based on the biological, language, cultural experiences, and personal experiences of that person.

Respect

After realizing that the difference between all people exists in such a deep and ingrained form, we need to develop respect for that difference. We need to realize that some characteristics of each mental model will remain the way they are, but others can and should be deconstructed, modified, and perfected. Whether it is to improve your relationship with yourself, with family, friends, co-workers, or clients.

Impacts At The Corporate Level

Primarily in the professional sphere, the awakening of self-knowledge, empathy and mutual respect, in the form of a strategic application, will achieve an organizational transformation that will begin in internal human relations and will reflect on the quality of corporate goals, objectives, and results.

In each mental model, there must be attitudes and thoughts that allow us to establish relations of mutual respect and to live in harmony with a greater number of people, even if the differences between all continue to exist. To exercise this understanding, it is valuable to experience other cultures; the different. After all, it is because of the differences that we have the opportunity to learn and evolve more each day.

Chapter 5 - What Are Your Mental Models And How Do They Affect Your Behavior?

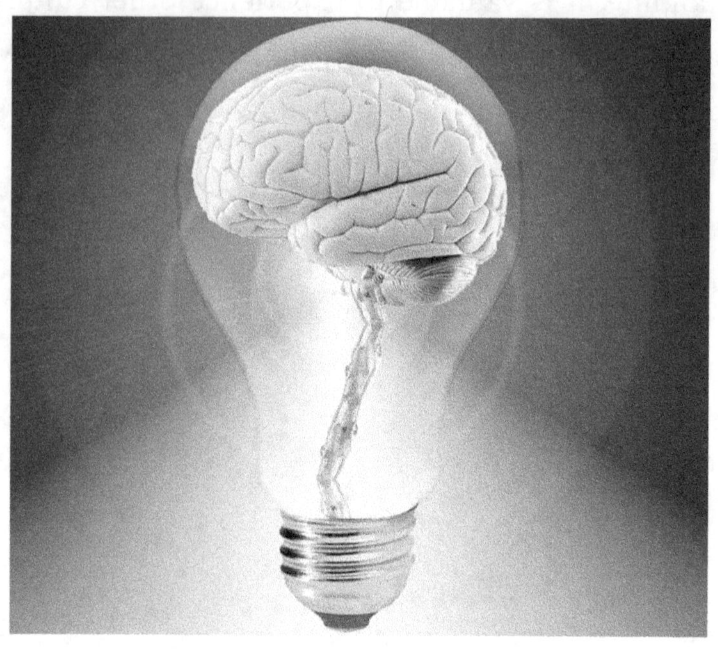

To start this topic and discuss the detailed reasons and consequences behind it, I would like to suggest a quick reflection: do you have any behavior that you do not like about yourself but that you cannot change? How many times have you gotten into situations where you would like to act differently? Have you ever wondered why it is so difficult to change behavior, even if it harms you in some way? Our behaviors are closely linked to our beliefs and often influence our way of acting and thinking, leading us to take action according to a pattern we have been given.

For example, you believe that being late is a lack of respect. And this generates in you the behavior of being always punctual. The writer Peter Senge, in The Fifth Discipline, defined mental models as "deeply rooted assumptions, generalizations, illustrations, images or stories that influence our way of understanding the world and acting on it." The mental model is not necessarily an absolute truth, but a truth created according to your beliefs, that is, what you believe influencing your behavior. Our mental models determine not only how we understand the world, but also how we act in it.

Another intriguing fact is that faced with the same situation, different people can behave in different ways, and this is directly linked to the mental models that each individual possesses. Recognizing a mental model and bringing it to consciousness is not an easy task, but it is necessary to help us understand how influenced we are by this pattern of thinking, that is, how we repeat certain behaviors in different situations. And it is important to remember that the same mental model can either limit us or push us toward goals or our personal identity.

Developing the best mental models possible to face any situation that presents itself is the key point to leverage the process of learning and development. Two skills may facilitate the process of identifying mental models: reflection and inquiry. 'Reflecting' refers to being aware of how mental models can affect our worldview; and 'inquiring' is about maintaining dialogues and interactions with others, sharing visions and experiences.

Reflection will bring the mental model to consciousness and questioning will help to determine if this is the best mental model to be used at that time if that mental model limits or leverages you towards your goals.

Mental Models and Decisional Processes

You do know now what a mental model is! Right? Yes, you are correct. It is our pattern of internal representations. It is the way we perceive the world, based on factors such as physiology, life experiences, and culture. So over time, we accumulate assumptions that define how we will experience our future experiences or perceive the world.

These mental models also have a very special impact on decision making. It is as if we have recorded patterns of behavior and principles used continuously in the analytical processes we have developed. We are programmed to respond to situations in a given way. This is beneficial because it usually speeds up the choice of a path. The question is, and when are our mental models no longer as effective as before?

Mental Renewal

Quick question: Is it wise to keep inflexible behavior in a change scenario? In the context of the choices we make, our mental models must be aligned with our needs and responsibilities. This means that priorities at the time of deciding may change, depending on the position and circumstances we experience.

In this way, without dynamism, we run the risk of continuing to apply obsolete mental models. It is dangerous to decide what to do in the future just based on the past, after all, like almost everything in life, something wonderful today can become old fashioned tomorrow.

Mental Models in Practice

Imagine that you worked for 5 years as a computer technician at a large infrastructure company. Your workload was gigantic, and you were responsible for almost everything, even for things outside of your training. You would do the job, issue your invoices, prospect new business, and take care of what happened.

In time you came to believe that you should handle everything, understand everything in detail, and not share your responsibilities with anyone. Basically, for 5 years, you were shaped to see yourself that way and believe that this was your mission in the organization.

However, one day, you received a promotion. You became an Infrastructure Project Manager. You don't take care of the technical part of a project anymore, but in its place, everyone is now answerable to you. Now tell me this, your growth in the responsibility of taking care of the details, being responsible for every bit of the activities and taking care of everything by yourself, are they still valid? Generally, no. Yes, only if you want to go crazy.

A new mental model became necessary, delegating. Maintaining the beliefs of the technician era would make your new state unfeasible. New decisions could no longer be taken by interpreting the world as before.

Make Reinvention a Lifestyle

Changes bring about imbalance, whether positive or negative. We tend to fight the imbalance to return to a stable position. Thus, fitting the mental models represents a counter-response to the changes we experience in any field of our lives.

Identify your mental models, understand if they are appropriate to your present moment, and reinvent yourself whenever necessary. Do not cling to the paradigms and constantly work the way you see the world. Renewing your interpretation of the facts can be the dividing line between success and failure.

Chapter 6 - Mental Models, Decision Making, and Business Planning

Due to the constant need to seek means to compete with well-structured and planned service projects, companies were forced to delineate plans and reflections in decision-making, focusing efforts on the process of analysis and reflection of standards mental health. To improve and direct their strategy, some companies adopt the Balanced Score Card (BSC) to improve their financial, organizational, customer expectations, and learning and growth prospects.

The competitiveness and productivity strategy tool results in an increase in the quality of services in the organizational environment. Including social processes in the company, such as job creation, health, and safety of its employees, are modern aspects in the management of many businesses.

The market is very competitive, and external actions such as quality and product improvement are not isolated as a competitive differential for competition because through benchmarking companies adopt the best practices in the market. Companies must also take into account advances in the internal environment by promoting improvements in the physical space, in the comfort and convenience of the clients, especially, to develop other capacities of their employees that not only the experience and the talent but also the self-knowledge, interpersonal competence, sensitivity and intuition, connectivity, versatility and adaptation.

There is no recipe for success if there is no change in the composition of the company. But the question is: where can I focus more on my strategy? It depends on who does it. It is necessary that the starting point for success is for the company to develop its strength and seek to solve its weaknesses.

How can one understand the attitudes of the individual? Does he already know? What does he understand, realize, what decisions he takes, how he behaves in an environment or task? At all times each of us makes different readings and interpretations of the world, people and situations, based on assumptions that shape our way of acting, our perceptions of reality (different from individual to individual).

The elements proposed to compose a profile of a successful mental model are: Values and moral principles: what one brings and leads to personal or professional life; Emotional Intelligence: Emotionally adjusted individuals have a greater perspective of experiencing satisfaction and tend to be more efficient in their path; Complex thinking: willingness to see things optimistically and relying on solutions appropriate to the circumstances, even the most complex; Linear or logical thinking: it eliminates double character and diversity;

Creativity: ability to develop creativity always seeking to be current and to seek information about everything that surrounds him, to be sensitive to all the events around him and curiosity to find what is hidden outside occurrences, elements and people; Capacity for Relationship and Communication: always seek the practice of self-knowledge and seek to develop collective skills, both for social and professional living. The main relationship of an individual begins in their family relationship that will shape their initial type of vision.

Mental Models, Decision-Making and Business Planning

According to Senge (1998), "Mental models are the means by which we interact with the world." The truth is that only the human mind is able to perceive the order of the universe. This is where one begins to question the effectiveness of knowing the individual in his personal or professional life. It is through the mental models of their managers and deputy managers that the strategies influence their teams in the present issues, in their internal aspects and in the variables of the external environment.

The approach in business management should be grounded with the style of leadership within a holistic view aimed at the organizational level, understanding how the parties relate. Mental Models can be said to refer to the way in which we use our already obtained knowledge to try to predict or presume the correct functioning of the component or aspect of the body world.

There has been a great revolution in the world since 1970, and we realize that more and more changes are occurring at an even greater speed. Today individuals are different from their ascendants and tend to see the world from another perspective; people are more educated, informed, communicative, and nonconformist, creating a new category in the world.

Today there are many successful professionals among corporate employees, liberals, academics, journalists, inventors and entrepreneurs with a new vision and perspective on what they think, feel and cry for jobs that have meaning, cherishing justice and rejecting intolerance, seeking happiness.

They are decision makers ready to execute effect tactics. The truth is that the world is undergoing global changes, and the professional has to be well corroborated and have a good understanding. Companies should consider better suited mental models and complement them with techniques and innovations that induce the development of these patterns.

Speaking in an internal environment, there are six elements that need to be worked very carefully: Strategy, Team, Culture, and Behavior, Politics, Processes, and Architecture.

Unfortunately, there are still obstacles in some companies in which the Mental Model is still from the past period, creating a barrier for some of these professionals.

The valuation of the human being by the company is essential for the development of the organization. The employee must be seen as a collaborator and be respected, with this, the effects become pretty evident: managers presenting results with less effort, having better strategic insights and being on the ethical side of things.

It can also be observed that there has recently been more competence in the organizational structure, in the principles of efficient production models and in the examples of quality and productivity. This evidence is seen in the hiring of skilled labor, which generates a positive factor in competitiveness among companies.

I believe that most managers and leaders are already beginning to realize that the most important material in your organization is the individuals who work in your organization, that is, your employees who help realize the company's goals. In order to increase its competitive advantage, the company must establish a performance standard for its actions in favor of quality and productivity.

Through communication and the ability to relate, organizations coupled with their managers, leaders, and teams are transforming their mental models into their decision-making, directing actions in the improvement of strategies of operability and competition with employee focus and investment in satisfaction and needs of its customers/consumers.

Mental Models and the Efficiency of Strategy

In the times we live, we are daily "bombarded" by innumerable information from all sides (news, internet, friends, parents, self-perception, etc.). Mental models are actually behavioral patterns, the reactions we have of, or the interpretations we make of, all that information that comes to us.

As children, we are "trainees" to perceive reality in the way the responsible ones do. That is why every city, state, or nation has a peculiar culture of its own. Culture is regional, family, and organizational are often imposed, offering us a pattern of acting, thinking, behaving, and so on. In companies, we can call these models or standards, Organizational Culture (general behavior pattern) and PARADIGMS (punctual patterns of perception in practice).

In the old days, we might believe that solutions to organizational problems could come in packages of closed and perfect management models bought at very high prices, but this paradigm has been broken for years because today we know that if we follow a single management model, our companies are doomed to fail. So we now believe that the interdisciplinary or multi-functionality of learning and tasks, both inside and outside the organization, is what is helping managers in making decisions and in the conception of strategic behaviors, given the complexity of thinking and the observance of the same in the organization, in view of the constant resolutions of human needs, that is, of the general needs of its employees and especially of its clients.

When we think of what is to be done for a company to succeed, the only conclusion is that hard thinking (or this, or that) no longer has nowhere near the same strength in industrial society as it used to have. The theories that are gaining strength in the contemporary world are those that take into account the diversity of thoughts and their complexity. Because we are linked to each other, diversified thinking becomes complex, in which it is understood that the relationships between individuals are inevitable, just as the influence we exert on each other is.

Human thought is complex and diverse since the same information can be absorbed in innumerable ways by the numerous interlocutors, precisely because each has its MENTAL MODEL. To make it clearer to understand what a "mental model" is, consider it as a "PROGRAM" in our brain, which has a database based on intellect (reasoning, interpretation, retention and analysis of facts), imagination (it is nourished by the perceptions of the intellect, it defines images and conceptions) and memory (it stores all that comes from the intellect and the imagination, aiding in the future redemptions of this information). That is why we are afraid of cockroaches, for example - the intellect perceives the cockroach, the imagination conceives the image and creates mental scenes of what this cockroach can do to us, triggering from memory similar situations occurred in the past, which will generate our reaction: kill the cockroach, run from it or be paralyzed.

Taking this into account, one can conclude that our brains have numerous programs - MENTAL MODELS - that trigger destructive or constructive behaviors. The fact that many do not know how to make money, maintain relationships, and even be productive at school or work comes from their MENTAL MODELS and can be explained perfectly by them.

For the implementation of a strategy, the manager must observe very well the MENTAL MODELS of his employees, in order to analyze if they are able to absorb the strategic guidelines of the company. In fact, this is one of the big problems companies face for the success of their strategies: the hurdles imposed by the team. So before seeking the implementation of a strategy, conduct an organizational climate survey to find out the strengths and weaknesses that can directly affect your company, work the motivation of employees, understand it, and respect it and their differences. But do not think that this is just for the employee to feel good in the company. It is also for another very important purpose – so that you, as the manager, with this information and sensations, can converge and manage the employees' "thoughts" for the success of the business strategy.

And this process is complex and constant because everything is in continuous movement, everything wants to adapt to a reality separately, and thoughts are one of those things that always try to adapt.

Chapter 7 - Think Fast And Think Slowly

Fast answer: What color is your refrigerator? What do cows drink?

If your answer to the second question was "milk," you have just discovered what heuristic availability is. Your system one of thinking, the fast system, has just given you a quick and wrong answer, based on the most accessible available information you have found. And now that you've stopped to think, your second system of thinking, the slow system, has just told you that what cows drink, in fact, is water.

In this silly little game are contained three very important concepts about the functioning of our brain and the way we make decisions on a day to day basis.

Two Systems

Have you ever found yourself driving and, without being sure of the reason, decided to change lanes quickly before another vehicle nearly hit you? If it had not changed lanes, an accident would have happened. But how did you react so fast? After the shock, your brain starts to get an explanation and maybe concludes that you are a great driver. I'm sorry to disappoint you, but this reaction you've had is very common. It's the result of many hours of driving experience. Your brain quickly interpreted several signals: the sound of the other car approaching too fast, the sound of the tires, a fleeting movement in the rearview mirror that does not match a car that goes straight, perhaps the movement of a third car that also avoided the accident, information stored in your subconscious that there was no one in the range to which you changed, knowledge of the responsiveness of your car engine, the sensitivity of the steering wheel, etc. All this and more was processed in a fraction of a second to take a very quick intuitive decision. The responsible for this impressive achievement is what psychologists call the system of thought.

System 1 is a very peculiar guy, always about to help us. It processes information extremely quickly and automatically, and makes decisions intuitively, without stopping to see if that decision is correct. All this without any sense of voluntary control. System 1 has helped us, during our time in cave dwellers, not so long ago, to understand that we should flee from dangerous animals that could eat us. It allows us to effortlessly carry out simple day-to-day tasks, such as:

- Coordinating hands and feet to drive a car
- Tell your fingers what movements to do on the computer keyboard to write this text.
- Interpret joy in someone's facial expression.
- Understand simple phrases in our mother tongue.
- Associate a certain accent with a cheerful personality.
- Solve the operation "2 + 2 = ..."?

Now answer the following question: What is the result of 32x19?

Unless you are a mathematical genius, you need at least to stop and think to perform the calculation in your mind, or perhaps with paper and pencil. What happens here is that System 1 has found a difficulty, a problem it cannot solve, and asks System 2 to take action. System 2 is very lazy. He is the one who has the last word always, but most of the time he accepts the decisions system 1 makes.

Back to the example of driving. You know that moment in the traffic where you control yourself, so you do not swear at the guy who almost hit your car? It was his system 2 taking over. Because System 2 is you. You (System 2) decided to handle yourself, despite the huge will (System 1) of cursing the other driver. And for that, it took a lot of effort because, as we said earlier, System 2 is lazy.

Daniel Kahneman explains the relationship between the two systems:

"System 1 is one that effortlessly generates impressions and feelings that are the main sources of explicit beliefs and deliberate elections of system 2. Automatic operations of system 1 generate patterns of ideas surprisingly complex, but only the slow system 2 can construct thoughts in an orderly series of steps".

To summarize: System 1 generates beliefs and suggests decisions based on these beliefs, and system 2 collects these decisions, accepts and executes them, except which system 1 has not been able to solve. Only in this case does system 2 make a slower and more thoughtful decision.

System 1 is the one in charge most of the time, solving problems quickly, making decisions effortlessly. And that works very well for us. Almost always. Because system 1 is responsible for all the psychological biases, it sometimes leads us to jump to conclusions and make wrong decisions. The problem is that it can not be disabled. It is always the first front line.

But if it is impossible to shut down system 1, how can we avoid all of our errors of judgment? How can I not curse the other driver? Using mental models.

Mental Models

As has been stated by me a thousand times up until now, a mental model is a representation of the world around us, in our minds. For example, the 4 seasons of the year are a mental model, a representation of how Earth changes climate throughout the year, depending on the distance from the Sun. If we see that the leaves of the trees are falling, we know that we are in the autumn, soon the weather will be colder, and we will need to get dressed. If we see that the flowers begin to appear everywhere, we know we are in the spring, and soon the heat will come.

Another more complex mental model is the Franklin effect. Benjamin Franklin once knew of a man who did not like him and had chosen him, Franklin, as an enemy. Then Franklin decided to settle the matter. For this, he went to the man and borrowed a book from his library. It was well known that Franklin's library was one of the best, and therefore Franklin's petition was received by the man as a great compliment. If Franklin, whose library was one of the best, was borrowing a book from him, it was because he appreciated and valued it. From that day on they were great friends until the end of their lives. Can you see the model? It can be applied to many situations in our lives. Franklin's reaction is not natural, it's a deliberate choice, after reflecting on the subject, and it takes a lot of effort. Asking a favor from someone who hates us is not easy.

Thinking this way, what is the only way to get our system 2 in control and stop us from cursing the driver of the other car? Reflecting before things happen, modeling the situation in our mind. If we reflect in advance on the fact that when a person cuts us off in traffic, our first act will be to curse him (this is the mental model), we will be prepared to identify the model when he introduces himself, and we can take control, with effort, and contain us.

In Investments, In Business, And In Life

Mental biases are innumerable, and when it comes to making investment or divestment decisions, they can make us go wrong in a catastrophic way. Selling a stock when it is falling without understanding the reason for the fall, or buying a stock when it is rising, without understanding the reason for the rise, are sure recipes for the disaster.

So one of our personal improvement goals should be (following Charlie Munger's suggestion) to create in our mind a lattice of mental models. A series of models, interwoven with each other like a trellis, to help us see the world in such a way that we can make better decisions every day, be better people and, ultimately, be and make those around us happier.

Continually in our daily lives, we make judgments that lead us to make wrong decisions. The origin of these errors and bad decisions lies in the way our mind is fast and efficient processing the information it receives. Although we cannot turn off our initial perceptions, we can prepare to pay attention to situations in which we know beforehand that we have a high probability of making a judgmental mistake. The way we do this is to study and learn as many mental models as possible, representations of the world that are in our mind.

The Paradox Of Choice – Having More Choices – Is It Really Good?

Have you ever had the feeling of being lost amid so many choices? Have you tried to buy a product and could not because you did not know which model was the most modern in the market? Have you ever been desperately trying to make your request at Spoleto, with so much pressure on what you would choose next?

And what about your daily basic decisions, what do you have to say? Which shoe did you choose to wear this morning? What task did you start first in your job? What clothes will you choose to go out tonight? Which most profitable investment fund are you going to invest?

If you stop to think, during your day, you make more choices than you realize. And this gets us pretty confused, does not it? Well, these are clear symptoms that there is a paradox of choice in your life. But what is this paradox?

Paradox of Choice

We always have the uncomfortable feeling that the product we have chosen from hundreds of options should be the perfect product. But we always realize that it was not. And this creates a degree of dissatisfaction, caused by the excess of items, models, options, etc. in the market. The more options we add to people's lives, the greater will be their expectations of meeting their need always to make the best choice.

However, having lots of choices produces paralysis instead of a sense of freedom. And even if we win the stage of paralysis and succeed in making the choice, we will be less satisfied with this option than if we had had fewer options to choose from.

The more buried we are in the options to choose from, the more emotional our decisions will become, based on brands, recommendations, striking slogans, affective memories, etc. Amidst more complicated decision-making, given the huge variety of items to choose from, our rational side ends up in the background.

Marketing Asthe Agent of Change

And it is there that we perceive the brand of the product as an important agent for breaking this barrier that the excess of choices can cause in the mind of the consumer. And it's easy to see the importance of good marketing strategies to introduce the brand, the logo, the slogan, etc., into the consumer's mind, in order to make them more loyal.

We can even say that the emotional side is fueled by this information that marketing reinforces every day in our minds. Therefore, the better the company's work in publicizing its brand and strengthening its position in the consumer's head, the easier it will be to make it decide by brand X, not the competitor's. And the greater the consumer identification with the brand, the more likely it is to buy other products from the same manufacturer in the next purchases.

At this point, however, it is important to emphasize that marketing is not always responsible for this achievement of the human mind. If the company in question does not develop good products, with innovative technologies and an offer of products and options that meet the demands of consumers, it will not do any good to have an excellent marketing campaign.

I believe you cannot speak in Paradox of Choice without mentioning Barry Schwartz, a psychologist and professor of Social Theory and Social Action at Swarthmore College in Pennsylvania, USA. He brought this discussion to light some years ago in his book "The Paradox of Choice: Why More Is Less."
In this book, the author addresses one of the great mysteries of modern life: why do individuals, even with so many choices never before seen, feel unhappy or confused when it comes to buying a product?

Reading this fantastic work is highly recommended for all marketing, management, and market intelligence professionals. He has also given several TED Talks on the same issue where he talks about this paradox and why he says that more is less?

As is mentioned in the book, Barry Schwartz contests the idea that more options of choice generate greater satisfaction. While he believes that it is interesting to exercise our freedom of choice, he believes that the sheer volume of choice is making people less happy and more anxious, leaving them more doubtful and therefore more frustrated.

"THE SECRET OF HAPPINESS IS LOW EXPECTATION" – BARRY SCHWARTZ

And in this myriad of often torturous choices, we end up wondering much more. Since the high number of questions ends up raising even more doubts about ourselves. We channel the justifications for our failures, or the bad choices we make, for the decisions we had to make when choosing X or Y to do. What if we had chosen option B? What would have happened?

When it comes to the variety of products on the market, we can say that our options are more and more similar. How many smartphones do you know that have 90% similar functions? How many tablets are coming on the market, almost like copies of each other? Choosing is getting harder and harder. According to Schwartz, there are four possible reasons for our dissatisfaction, or unhappiness, when making a decision based on infinite possibilities of choice. They are:

1) The cost of opportunity: In a scenario where there are several options to choose from, we will invariably have to choose one option over the other. There is no way we can choose a perfect product in most cases, so we always have to live with the concept of opportunity cost. Where we choose an item by its qualities, on condition that we give up the benefits of the other item.

2) Repentance: This is a concept that accompanies any kind of decision, especially if you have questions about what you are choosing. Even more so if we take into account that the simple act of not choosing is already, in itself, a choice. In this way, repentance arises from what we fail to choose as well.

3) Adaptability. Today we chose product B because we think it's better than product F. But if tomorrow the manufacturer launches an upgraded F product with more features and options to choose from, you'll probably have questions about the decision you made today. Our need to always have the most updated products on the market can harm us in a way.

4) The weight of the comparison. It's the old story of always thinking that the neighbor's grass is always greener than ours. We are all the time comparing ourselves to our friends, co-workers, family, etc. And the time to choose a product is no different.

In one of his studies, psychologist Barry Schwartz divided consumers into two distinct categories, the maximizers, and the satisfiers. Maximizers, according to him, seek at any cost the most advantageous option. They are those people who go through all the available stores in search of a shirt with the best cost/benefit. Satisfactors, on the other hand, feel happy and satisfied with the first option they find and that fully satisfy their need. As soon as they like a product, they soon stop looking for better or more complete ones. It's easy to imagine which of the two groups tends to be less happy in their buying decisions, is not it? Those who always seek to compare and contrast: the maximizers.

Do you agree that having too many choices is worse for the consumer? Or do you believe that having many options to choose is part of the evolution of the market and systematic decision-making? Think, talk, and discuss it.

Learn To Develop Your Lateral Thinking

It happens frequently. When we have to face a more or less difficult problem, we always begin to doubt ourselves by thinking that it will be very difficult to find the solution. The great contribution of lateral thinking is its simplicity, its originality, and its creativity. And let us remember: the first thing to clarify is that everything, absolutely everything, is easier than we think.

Perhaps one of the main mistakes we usually make is to use too much so-called linear thinking, that is, one that uses logic in an express and unidirectional sense for a single conclusion. On the other hand, lateral thinking is free and imaginative, and with it, we can count on infinite ways of obtaining one or even several solutions.

Learning to Be Creative

The so-called "lateral thinking" was so termed by Edward de Bono, an Oxford psychologist who wanted to come up with a new way of solving problems and facing challenges. A perspective that allows us to move to all sides and not just in a straight line, which allows us to be provocative and to go through less obvious ways, stimulating our mind and learning in the same process.

The importance of lateral thinking has acquired a relevant weight in the field of social and individual psychology. Particular value is given to the fact that people can be original in their reasoning away from the common or expected. In order for us to achieve this freedom and originality in our daily reasoning, we can use the following techniques:

1. Random ideas: An essential component of lateral thinking is to have an open mind. This implies not to stick to a specific option. Moreover, it would be advisable to think of new random

ideas and options, however strange or discordant, to find solutions to our problems.

2. Use analogies: analogies serve to compare ideas that seemingly have nothing to do with each other. The purpose is to get away from the stereotypes, from the expected or from the boxed. Consider the famous drawing of the play "The Little Prince." Is it a hat? Is it a snake that swallowed an elephant? Is it an elephant under a hat?

3. Method of inversion: a risky technique, no doubt. When we have a problem or a challenge to deal with, what if we analyze it in reverse? When we dissect a problem, new paths may appear that we did not expect. Thinking the opposite of what we have pre-established can bring us innovative visions that not everyone is able to see.

4. Fractionation or division: The purpose of this proposal is to subdivide the problem into smaller parts to see the challenge in a broader way with each and every one of your options. Mental blocks usually come when we see only part of the challenge or problem. However, every act is made up of small parts that we must take into account.

In order for us to put these ideas into practice, let us look at some of the little puzzles that surround "Lateral Thinking." Try to think of them by applying the strategies we recommended earlier. You'll see that these are seemingly simple challenges, but the question will surely baffle you. First remember the most important principle of lateral thinking: everything is much easier than we think.

* Puzzle 1. "There are six eggs in a basket. Six people take one egg each. How is it possible that in the end there is still an egg in the basket? "

* Puzzle 2." Grandpa was having breakfast, and inadvertently, his glasses fall into the coffee cup. When he pulled them out from inside the cup, he realized that they had not gotten wet. How can this be? "

* Puzzle 3." How can a bladder be pierced without air escaping and without the bladder making a noise? "

* Puzzle 4." There are three elephants bathing in a tank one meter and a half deep. How do you think they'll get out of the water when they're done? "

How To Define Goals?

The goals that are defined organizationally may have different interests or may have been described from different points of views than what the organization plans to achieve, for example, in market share, growth, billing, positioning against policies or image, profitability, etc.

You can also set goals to achieve internal changes, such as the expansion of the staff, the improvement of the work environment, the efficiency of operating expenses or simply to raise the morale of employees. Organizations must define, as we have been reporting, goals that represent their identity and future, and these must be correctly defined so that they can be achieved. If you consider how to define objectives and goals for your organization, start by clarifying your priorities and the direction you want to take them.

It is here where it is suggested that when defining goals/objectives, a standard of this activity is used, which is the use of the rule SMART. The SMART rule is named after the initials in English of Specific (specific), Measurable (measurable), Achievable (achievable), Realistic (realistic), and Time-Bound (limited in time).

If you are considering defining objectives and goals for your organization, start by clarifying your priorities and the direction you want to take them. Then work with the SMART rule defining them:

S-Specific means that we must define our goals/objectives clearly and identifying what we want to achieve.

M-Measurable, the defined goals/objectives should be measurable through key performance indicators (KPIs) to determine their efficiency.

A-Achievable, we must bear in mind that each of the goals/objectives that we define must be framed in the reasonableness of the compliance, that is, it must be within the possibilities of the staff and the budget allocated. Few things are more demotivating for the employees of an organization than facing goals that are impossible to achieve, either due to lack of budget, empower, dedication, skills, and/or insufficient planning.

R-Relevant, the goals/objectives must be contributors "without equa non" to the strategic plan that the organization has defined, otherwise it is very likely that we need to review them, since the organization sets its mission and vision through said plan and if the intermediate actions do not direct their results towards that focus, they are probably not so important.

T-Time, every objective/goal must be contained in a specific time of achievement. Otherwise, it is impossible to track and measure them, and they usually end up squandering efforts and resources if this definition is not clear and concise. The definition of the times must take into consideration that some goals/objectives are the results of achievements of others that precede them, which is why it is important to foresee this when a term of compliance is assigned.

Finally, How Can I Make Sure, I Have Optimal Goals/Objectives?

There is no rule that guarantees that my goals are the right ones and neither can it be assured that those that I have considered correct for a moment of my life or organization remain in that status all the time.

Both the goals and the results that you aspire to achieve (measurable through KPI - Key Performance Indicator) must be monitored periodically to know how close or far from them you are. As Peter Drucker said, "As important as setting goals is to be able to measure them in their evolution since it is not possible to control or improve something that is not measured."

Organizational goals are not a "commodity" that can be copied or extrapolated from one organization to another; they are specific to each organization at a specific time and under special conditions that must be surveyed and taken into consideration at the time of implementation and follow-up.

To be successful, the goals depend not only on having been correctly defined (respected the SMART model detailed above), but they must be led by the high organizational management.

There must also be a team with the necessary conditions to carry them forward and, in all cases, the goals must be fully aligned with the strategic objectives / strategic plan of the organization.

Therefore, we always say that to achieve our goals it is essential to follow these steps: define the correct goals (preferably based on the SMART rule), assign them to the appropriate collaborators, measure them periodically and evaluate their compliance. If the goals are not being met, the organization with critical authority must understand why this is happening and, if necessary, make the operational/strategic adjustments necessary to achieve them. If this were not enough, it might be time to rethink the defined goals.

After having defined my annual goals/objectives, it becomes almost as critical as having the task of communication towards our work teams, defining their minor objectives and their respective KPIs. In this way, the partial fulfillment of the goals of the most operative employees will be the basis for achieving global compliance with the goals and objectives of the entire organization.

Does Achieving These Goals Guarantee Success?

Unfortunately the answer to this question is "not always", since it is possible that the goals have not been defined correctly, that the conjuncture of the micro or macroeconomy has changed, that the legislation that existed or a new one that was sanctioned modify the Legal "status quo" of the country, or that several of these conditions have occurred together generating new scenarios that do not allow one to achieve what was planned. Therefore, we can assert that the definition of goals will not guarantee success. However, I would dare to say that, in parallel, it is almost impossible to be successful without the construction of goals that define the direction of my organization.

Chapter 8 – Cognitive Bias - Concept, What It Is, Meaning

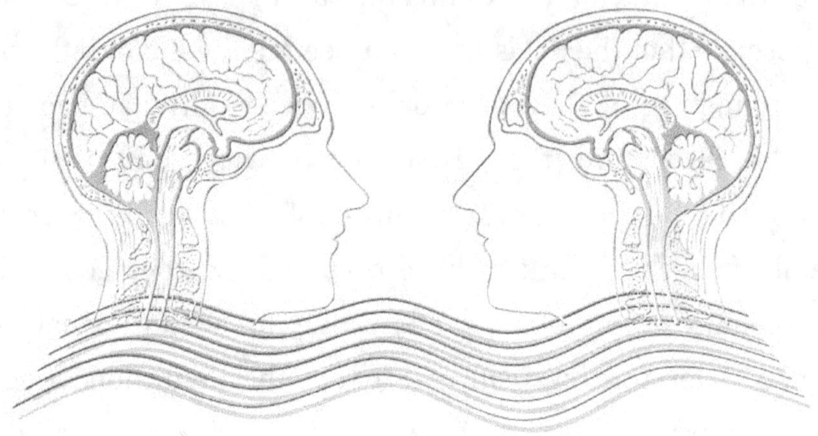

The functioning of the human mind is one of the great enigmas of humanity. We have a pretty rough idea of our rational mechanisms, but these are not the only ones that operate when making decisions.

Behavior specialists know that when it comes to establishing behavioral strategies, we also use imperfect mental processes, self-concepts, and ideas that are contrary to rational thinking. These mechanisms of the mind are known as cognitive bias. It can be said that these are unconsciously used psychological tricks. Cognitive biases are mental shortcuts that often lead us to make wrong decisions. We seek information that confirms our initial expectations or personal beliefs, as well as avoiding any information that may contradict us.

We often assume in an unjustified way that other people think like us. In other words, we project evaluations and personal ideas about others. As a general rule, we opt for proposals that provide us with immediate gratification, and we give up those in the medium and long term, even though we know they can be beneficial to our interests. We mistakenly assume that the events of the past were predictable (in this case, we speak of the bias of retrospective understanding).

We give more importance to possible losses than to possible gains.

We tend to think that we know others better than ourselves.

We give more importance to the initial information about something and forget the rest of the information.

When we are faced with attractive people, we attribute certain qualities that are not necessarily right.

We think something is good because so many individuals believe.

Appreciating Conclusions

The main feature of any cognitive bias is its appearance of rationality. These shortcuts or mental self-deceptions constitute false illusions because, in all, there is a change in the information process. Knowledge of these mental mechanisms is used in the world of marketing and in the political sphere (the various forms of populism are based largely on the use of messages that "touch the fiber" of some cognitive bias). From the individual point of view, knowing the cognitive biases helps us to know why we act in a certain way

Learn How to Make Better Decisions: Avoid Cognitive Biases

Making decisions in the corporate environment is no easy task. We are often faced with challenges that require quick, assertive attitudes. But when do these decisions define profound changes? Are you hitting? What if I told you that your biggest enemy in this process is yourself? Or rather, your mind!

Here, I will try to explain some cognitive biases that mask our decision-making and make us think we are on the right track. Understand and learn how to validate such behaviors so that your decisions are correct and assertive.

Understanding the Biases

We receive thousands and millions of quanta of information constantly. Our brain is stimulated every second by different sources. And to deal with this myriad of messages, our mind triggers a kind of "shorter way" for decision making and completion for some types of problems.

Called Heuristics, these types of cognitive biases are mental shortcuts that cause us to act simply and instinctively in certain situations without having to reach the deepest levels of thought. This mechanism was developed thousands of years ago when human ancestors did not have much time to deeply analyze situations before acting.

However, today, in order to make intelligent and assertive decisions, it is essential that the situation, the context, the possibilities, and those involved are analyzed objectively. That is, it is necessary to know how to avoid these shortcuts. In the organizational environment, a good leader is one who, even under pressure, can avoid easy and instinctive solutions. It is the one that reflects, looks for external information, understands situations, and evaluates the best way to act.

Now that you have a better understanding of what cognitive biases are and how they work, here are some of the types that can hinder the quality of your decision making.

Confirmation Bias

Do you know when we are sure of something, and we can verify by our own experiences or by information obtained without further research? Often we are stubborn with ideas without concrete foundations, without a real sample. We simply believe because we want to believe, without worrying about really true explanations.

Process of Confirmation Bias

This type of mindset is known as Confirmation Bias and goes beyond a stubborn personality. This mental shortcut deceives us and makes us look for information that confirms what we want to prove, that is, our pre-established perceptions and biased assumptions.

I'll explain better. Thinking about the debate on the regulation of the use of weapons, for example, let's suppose that Peter supports control of the sale and use of weapons. Therefore, he tends to seek information and opinions that confirm his belief. And when he learns of incidents involving weapons, he interprets this in favor of his hypothesis and argues that if there was a limitation in the sale, perhaps it would have been avoided. But Felipe, on the other hand, has the opposite view and is in favor of facilitating the legal arms trade. Therefore, he looks for information that proves his theory and not the contrary. And when he learns of the same cases as Peter, he asserts his hypothesis and says that if there were a release, other civilians could interfere with that incident if they had weapons as well.

This case shows two opposing opinions on the same subject and interpretations favorable to their respective theories. And even having access to the same events, they tend to draw conflicting conclusions, confirming their own beliefs. Even though it seems simple to identify, this type of bias exposes something natural of the human species: we are more likely to look for data and information that confirm what we want to prove, rather than seeking arguments that refute our initial hypothesis.

It is very important to identify and avoid this kind of mental process so that a situation is widely understood so that you can make a good decision. For this, we need to constantly question ourselves, always seeking to understand all the real facts that prove our "certainties" and, especially, the reason why we believe in that.

Conformity Bias

In another sense, there is a distinct characteristic of the human being, as a social agent, which is to be influenced directly by the masses. That is, when inserted into a particular group, we are more predisposed to act according to the majority's choices, even if this breaches some belief or personal judgment.

Illustration of Conformity Bias

Psychology classifies this kind of mental shortcut as Conformity Bias, which makes us adapt to situations and beliefs according to the environment in which we operate.

For example, let's imagine that Luiza goes through a selective process and soon begins to experience the organizational culture of the new job. According to her perception in the early days, the company has a great failure in the part of the orientation and training of employees. But, conversing with colleagues and leaders on the subject, she finds that most believe that this problem does not exist, quite the contrary. So, even if you do not agree, it will hardly openly expose your opinion, for fear of going against the majority opinion.

This bias represents the famous saying of "dancing according to music." It is the art of trying not to be the exception to the rule, not to stand out "negatively." It is a natural fear caused by our mind, which can lead us to make bad decisions, just because it seems to agree with what most people believe especially if this effect causes opinions to be suppressed.

Therefore, it is worth stressing that a truly transparent environment takes into account diverse opinions and points of view, regardless of who the issuer is. This all makes the decisions that are taken, fairer, more thoughtful, and more efficient.

In the corporate environment, it is imperative to know how to avoid this bias. It is necessary to go against the flow, to try to be authentic and to remain firm to its values, independent thoughts, creativity, and its own characteristics. Encouraging always the good use of constant feedback. After all, as Jim

Hightower put it, "The opposite of courage is not cowardice, its compliance. Even a dead fish can go according to the flow. "

Surviving Bias

Who has never sought inspiration from such personalities as Mandela, Bill Gates, Walt Disney, Oprah or Roger Federer? All of these have inspiring life stories, in fact. But paying attention only to these people can be a great trap of our mind.

It's easy to focus on success, right? The Survivor Bias shows that we tend to look only to those people who have been very successful, even if the path has been long. At first, wanting to mirror stories of success and victory can be motivating. However, it is worth mentioning that many other people, who are not in the spotlight, also have much to teach us.

What often lies beneath the cloth is that these people who are victorious and considered inspiring, are the exception to the exception. That portion of 1 in 1 billion in the world that really manages to overcome gigantic challenges. And when we are inspired by them, we forget that people who are not so good or even fail, show that success does not have a single path.

It is not a matter of being negative or not looking for bigger things. It's just to consider a number of examples (from successes to failures) to be more likely to make good decisions about how to follow your dreams.

What worked for Steve Jobs is not going to work for you. But, many other cases can also help you understand what went right or wrong so that you try to achieve your success.

This bias makes your mind hide you from failure and focus only on success. But a very important point to achieve what you want is precisely to understand the difference between what is to fail and what is to be successful. So that you are motivated, but knowing what you need to face.

Overcoming Mental Shortcuts

It is very important to know and be able to diagnose the biases that hinder your decision making, and it is also necessary to be clear on how to solve these problems. Regardless of the bias, you are experiencing; a good solution is always to try to look at the situation with a more holistic and complete view. It is to follow the step by step: stop, take a step back, analyze, understand, make the right decision, and move on.

It is necessary to understand that sometimes we have a certain type of reasoning in our minds, which results in making a particular choice easier. Now, this may be because we want it to be so, because it is more comfortable to go according to what others think, or because it worked for someone else. But it is imperative to look at whether that situation really conforms to what you need to decide.

It is simply acting cool, smart, and keeping your feet on the ground, focusing on what is real. Therefore, always reflect on the reasons why you are making a decision. Is it in accordance with reality? What are the contrary opinions? Who will be affected? Is the idea of the majority really what I believe? What are the positive and negative examples that I should consider? In this way, with a more analytical and broad vision, making good decisions will be much simpler. Do not give room for your mind to disturb you! Use it as best as you can, even because the thousands of cognitive biases that exist are very important for our mind to function. The important thing is to understand at what point this is going to harm you.

I recently read a very cool post on the cognitive bias on the site Beyond the Roadmap; it was a translation of Buster Benson's article where a series of biases were listed that affect our decisions and judgments, inspired by them I decided to do a book about the subject.

We are always choosing! We are always under the responsibility of making choices (from the simplest to the most complex). We decide, for example, if we are going to start reading an article and go to the end, or if we stop reading and we will see some fun video that they send us. We choose whether we are going to do the activities we plan or whether we will procrastinate a little bit more. We chose to eat a sweetmeat instead of strictly maintaining the diet. Every day we have to make so many choices, and we are already so used to it that we barely realize that we have made a choice.

A film that shows very well the relationship between small - and even big choices - and its results is the movie "Black Mirror: Bandersnatch."

Whether you like it or not, that movie makes us - for a while - wake up to a fact:
Everything in life is a matter of choice. Sure, life is full of choices - from the simplest to the most complex - but most of our choices are not as rational as we think. We are not so rational because (to paraphrase Drummond):

"There was a bias in the middle of the road; at the halfway point, there was a bias."

In the path of our decisions, we are influenced by an infinity of cognitive biases. But they are basically distortions that happen in our perception, making us judge situations in a not very rational way, automating most of our choices and judgments.

Cognitive biases exist for a few reasons. We spend a lot of energy as we need to think about a subject. This is because a choice results in several consequences and is the result of several factors. So, we can say that they exist to solve a (or some) major problem(s).

Excessive information; lack of meaning; need to act quickly and to know what needs to be remembered in future situations.

Problem # 1 - Too much information. We are constantly receiving a multitude of information. When we are watching television, we are receiving information; when we are having casual conversations with friends, we are receiving information; when we are receiving WhatsApp messages or rolling our Facebook Feed, we are receiving information. Working rationally every information we receive would be extremely tiring, it's completely impractical. To deal with a large amount of information and give more importance to the specific facts, we have some biases.

1. We attach more importance to the details that are already implicit in our memory - or are repeated very often. This rule is simple and very easy to notice. Think:

- Why do the songs which are more chatty and repeated never leave our head?
- Why do companies invest in slogans and jingles for their products?

I had a history teacher in high school who repeated religiously three times everything I considered important to highlight. No wonder all the students complained about this didactic and even played, but the notes of the tests showed something impressive: the knowledge was impregnated in our heads.

Availability Heuristics: This is a cognitive bias where people predict the likelihood of something happening according to how easily they can remember this phenomenon.

Attention bias: Attention bias occurs when a person does not take into account all information related to a choice and only pays attention to some associations and correlations when making a judgment.

Cascade of availability: A repeated lie several times becomes true? Perhaps! This is a self-sustaining process where majority belief gains more relevance by increasing its repetition in public discourse.

Effect of mere exposure: When some image appears with a certain frequency, we tend to feel more familiar with it, causing a comforting effect in relation to what it represents. We tend to develop greater affection for this image.

Dependent forgetfulness of tips: It is the difficulty to remember what has no tips to be evoked. We tend to remember better things that have associations with other memories.

Context effect: The learning context influences our memory. A very common example is when you revisit a place where you spent your childhood and remember experiences that lived in those days.

Memory mood bias: People's emotional or mental state can also facilitate memory access.

Frequency illusion / Baader-Meinhof Phenomenon: This is the phenomenon in which people who have just learned or perceived something begin to see related things everywhere.

Empathy Gap: Occurs when the influence of the emotional state (hot-cold) is underestimated before a judgment.

Bias of Omission: What is worse? Committing a crime or seeing a crime being committed - and with the possibility of repeating itself over and over again - and being oblivious to what is happening? The bias of omission makes us see the omission of something harmful as something much less serious than a wrong practice.

2. Funny / visually attractive / bizarre and anthropomorphic elements attach more than non-bizarre and non-comical elements. Our brains tend to give more importance to the facts that stand out from what is common, just as we ignore what is considered common or expected.

Bizarre effect: The tendency we have to give to bizarre events is more important.

Von Restorff Effect: This effect determines that when in contact with several different stimuli, we tend to pay more attention to those that are most different from the others.

Effect of the superiority of figures: Figures, photographs, and images are more easily remembered than words.

Effect of self-awareness: This is the tendency for people to remember information according to how they feel involved.

Negativity bias: A negative event has greater weight and relevance in people's memory than positive and neutral events.
3. We notice when something has changed. And we constantly judge based on their contrasts and differences. We also tend to make comparisons of similar things.

Anchoring or Focalism: The tendency to attach greater importance to the first information received.

Contrast Effect: Refers to the increase or decrease of cognition or perception that is the result of an immediately preceding or simultaneous exposure to a minor stimulus.

Effect of denomination (or the illusion of money): The tendency to think of money in nominal rather than real terms. For example, poker chips are worth money. However, the fact that chips are wagered - not paper money - makes people feel less betting.

Framing effect: The way a situation is shown directly influences our judgment.

Weber-Fechner's Law: Refers to the relationship between the intensity and the perception of the change of a stimulus.

The bias of distinction: It tends to prefer to evaluate two options as opposites than when evaluating them separately.

4. The details that confirm our beliefs are always the most attractive! Our attention will always turn more to those situations which we are more sympathetic to. We ignore concepts that contradict our beliefs because rethinking concepts is very costly to our brains.

Confirmation evidence bias: Tendency to seek information that corroborates our lines of thought.

Congruence bias: Tendency to test hypotheses directly instead of testing alternative hypotheses.

Post-purchase rationalization: Tendency to justify our spending even though they are irrational.

Pro-choice bias: Tendency to retroactively assign a good judgment to the choice made.

Selective perception: Tendency not to observe or quickly forget negative things related to our positions. For example, when we like a person who makes a mistake, we tend to judge him less than if we were a person we do not know by making the same mistake.

Expectation-observer effect: Trend of influence on the part of the researcher when interpreting results. The possibility for a researcher to unconsciously influence the outcome of their research, moving toward confirmation of evidence.

Ostrich Effect: Tendency to ignore negative news about our judgments and/or choices.

Subjective validation: subjective validation - or Forer effect, or Barnum effect - it is the tendency that we have to believe that events without any logical connection can have some kind of connection according to our beliefs.

A very common example is the people's belief in astrology - nothing against it,but, I find the subject very amusing.

Semmelweis effect: Tendency to reject new evidence or new knowledge because it contradicts established norms, beliefs, or paradigms.

Problem # 2 - Lack of meaning. We will never know about everything around us, and it is often demanded that we know about something so that we can make a decision. How do I do if I have to decide something I know little or nothing about? Cognitive biases are also good for this!

1. We find stories similar to those we know and patterns which are familiar.We may not have lived 0.0000001% of the stories we heard, but our tendency will be to look for similarities with what we already know so we can have the power to judge or choose on a certain subject.

Confabulation: This is a memory error defined as the production of false and distorted memories about yourself or other people/things without the clear intention of self-deception.

Grouping illusion: The tendency to give an event grouping a correlation that does not actually exist based on isolated observations.

Insensitivity to sample size: Tendency to judge the probability of obtaining a sample statistic without respecting sample size.

Anecdotal Fallacy: Tendency to use a single experience of your own or someone else's example as a solid and compelling argument.

Expiration of validity: Excessive self-confidence in predicting and analyzing a data set.

Masked Man Fallacy: Occurs when someone makes the wrong use of Leibniz's law to construct their arguments.

The illusion of the recent: Tendency to believe that a term or word recently used is new, when in fact it has been around for a long time.

Gambler's fallacy: Also known as Monte Carlo fallacy is the fallacy that if something has happened all too often now, the future trend is that it will continue to be frequent (vice versa).

Hot hand: Believe that by experiencing a good result, the tendency is to achieve the same performance in the future.

Correlation illusion: It is the phenomenon of the perception of a relationship between variables (typically people, events, or behaviors), even when there is no such relationship.

Pareidolia: Tendency to observe vague stimuli and assign meanings that go against what is known by the observed ones, for example, to see animals in the clouds.

Anthropomorphism: Anthropomorphism is the attribution of human traits, emotions, or intentions to nonhuman entities. Do you know that person who speaks for the pet as if he has human feelings?

2. We fill in characteristics of stereotypes, generalizations, and past histories whenever there are new instances or voids of information. When we have limited information about something/someone, our brain tends to compose what we lack information with our hunches or from people close to whom we trust.

Group assignment error: Tendency to believe that the individual choice of a person reflects the decision of the group to which it belongs or the tendency to believe that the position of a group concerns the individuals that integrate it.

Intragroup favoritism: The tendency to see with more affection the practices and characteristics of the people who are part of the same groups that we participate in.

Stereotyping: Generalizations that seek to aggregate a set of factors and direct them to a particular group.

Essentialism: It is the view that every entity has a set of attributes that are necessary to its identity and function.

Functional fixation: Cognitive bias that limits us to using objects only in the ways in which they are conventionally used.

Effect of credibility: Tendency to give yourself much credibility and security in your self-image and self-concept.

Fair world hypothesis: The belief that a person's actions are inherently inclined to bring morally just and appropriate consequences to that person.

Argument from Fallacy: The tendency to consider a completely incorrect argument for containing a fallacy.

Authority bias: Tendency to attribute more validity to what authority says and inclination to be more easily influenced by it.

Automation bias: Propensity to favor automated decision-making system suggestions and ignore contradictory information made without automation, even if they are correct

Adhesion effect: The more people believe in something / do something, the more people adhere to belief or behavior.

Placebo Effect: It is a substance or treatment without the intended therapeutic value.

3. We imagine that elements and persons with whom we are familiar or have affection as better than elements or persons with whom we are unfamiliar or carry no affection.

Halo Effect: Tendency to assign judgments to people/things/groups/places according to some stereotyped characteristics.

Intra-group favoritism: A pattern that favors the people in the group to the detriment of people from other groups.

Group assignment error: The mistake in assigning similarities between two or more people outside our group, distancing ourselves to the maximum of them.

Racial effect: The tendency to recognize more easily the faces of the breed with which one is more familiar (which is more often the breed itself).

Cheerleader Effect: It is the cognitive bias that leads us to believe that individuals are more attractive when they are in a group.

Known road effect: A trend where travelers will estimate the time it takes to travel the routes differently, depending on their familiarity with the route. Frequently traveled routes are evaluated as having less time than unknown routes.

Reactive value decrease: A tendency to devalue a proposal that comes out of an "enemy" / a person we do not like.

4. We simplify probabilities and numbers to make it easier to think about them.

Mental Accounting: It is money being assigned to certain "responsibilities" rather than being viewed as fungible. For example, most people, while buying something in installments by a credit card, do not consider the interest, they only consider if they will have the money to pay the monthly installments.

Bias of normalcy: It is a belief that people have when considering the possibility of a disaster. This causes people to underestimate both the likelihood of a disaster and its possible effects because people believe that things will always work out as things normally have.

Fallacy to the appeal of probability: Belief to consider something guaranteed due to its probability - or possibility.

Murphy's Law: Belief that if something can go wrong, it will go wrong.

Fallacy of conjunction: It is the tendency to judge the probability that the whole is less than the probabilities of the parts. For example, a tendency to believe that a woman is likely to be assaulted on the street is more likely to be robbed on the same street.

Survival bias: The logical mistake of focusing on people or things that have gone through some selection process and ignoring those who did not. This happens a lot when we see stories of overcoming, and we are inspired.

Zero-sum bias: The zero-sum bias describes intuitively judging that a situation is zero-sum (that is, the resources earned by one part are matched by losses corresponding to another part) when in fact it is a sum other than zero.

Effect of denomination: The tendency to spend more money when denominated in small amounts.

Miller's Law: Most people store 7 (+ or - 2) information items in short-term memory. Thus, our short-term memory comprises 5 to 9 items.

5. We think we know what others are thinking. We tend to believe that people know what we know or think as we think.

Curse of knowledge: Difficulty in communicating effectively with people who do not have the same level of knowledge about something, assuming that everyone has the same understanding.

Transparency illusion: Tendency to overestimate the degree to which your personal mental state is known to others. "How did my best friend not notice that I was bad??"

Spotlight effect: Tendency to believe that you are being noticed more by others than you are.
External agent illusion: It is a set of attribution biases consisting of illusions of influence, insight, and benevolence, proposed by Daniel Gilbert, Timothy D. Wilson, Ryan Brown, and Elizabeth Pinel.

Asymmetric perception illusion: Tendency to believe that we know people better than themselves.

Extrinsic incentive bias: Extrinsic incentive bias is an attributional bias according to which people attribute relatively more "extrinsic incentives" (as a monetary reward) than "intrinsic incentives" (such as learning a new skill) by weighing the of others instead of themselves.

6. We design our current mental assumptions and models in the past and in the future.

Bias of hindsight: The retrospective bias, also known as the know-it-all phenomenon or creeping determinism, refers to the common tendency of people to perceive events that had already occurred as having been more predictable than before events occurred.

- "I already knew that was going to happen!"
- "Why did not you warn me?"

Bias of the result: An error made in the evaluation of something in view of its result. Specifically, outcome bias occurs when the same behavior produces more ethical condemnation when it produces a poor outcome, rather than a good one, even if the outcome is determined by chance.

Moral luck: Moral fortune describes the circumstances in which a moral agent receives moral guilt or praise for an action or its consequences, even though it is clear that this agent has no complete control over the action or its consequences.

Decline: The strong belief that society or an institution tends to decline. This predisposition is related to the pink retrospective cognitive bias that sees the past more favorably and the future as negative. "It was good before."

Telescope effect: Tendency to temporal distortion of reality, seeing events closer as distant or more distant as near.

Promising Retrospective / Pink Retrospective: Tendency to see the past as more favorable and the future as a bad thing.

Bias of impact: It is the tendency of people to overestimate the duration or intensity of future emotional states.

Bias of pessimism: The bias of pessimism is an effect in which people exaggerate the likelihood that negative things will happen to them.

Planning fallacy: It is a phenomenon in which predictions about how much time it will take to complete a future task show a bias of optimism and underestimate the time required.

Time-bias: Time-saving bias describes the tendency of people to misjudge the time that can be saved (or lost) by increasing (or decreasing) speed. "If I do not sleep tonight doing the work, I'll be done tomorrow."

Pro-innovation bias: A pro-innovation bias is a belief that innovation must be adopted by society as a whole without the need for change or adjustment.

Projection bias: Projection bias is the tendency to falsely project current preferences into a future event.

Limitation bias: Tendency to overestimate your ability to control impulsive behavior.

Problem # 3 - Need to act fast.

There is a demand for quick action in many areas of our lives. With the scarcity of information and the time we need to take certain measures as quickly as possible, what does it take for us to have the confidence and the attitude to act quickly?

1. To act, we need to be confident in our ability to impact and feel that what we do is important. It is very important that we have confidence - and even the courage that only overconfidence can give - to act quickly.

Overconfidence effect: This cognitive bias causes people to overvalue themselves in some situation, not taking into account other crucial factors involved, ignoring the risks of the decision.

Egocentric bias: egocentric bias is the tendency to rely too much on our own perspective and/or to have a higher opinion about ourselves than about reality.

Bias of optimism: Tendency not to believe in the probability of suffering a negative consequence.

Social desirability: Respond to situations in a way that is better evaluated by other people.

Third-person effect: Tendency to believe that media have a greater influence on others than on oneself. Believe that it is less influenced by biases that affect everyone.

Forer / Barnum effect: It is the tendency that we have to believe that events without any logical connection can have some kind of connection according to our beliefs.

Illusion of control: Tendency to overestimate your ability to have events under control.

Effect of False Consensus: A tendency for people to believe that their beliefs, values, habits, and opinions reflect the thinking of most people.

Dunning-Krueger Effect: It is a cognitive bias in which people of low ability have illusory superiority and misjudge their cognitive ability as being greater than it.

Difficult-easy effect: It is a cognitive bias that manifests itself as a tendency to overestimate the probability of success in a task perceived as difficult and to underestimate the probability of success in a task perceived as easy.

Illusion of superiority: It is a cognitive bias condition in which a person overestimates their own qualities and abilities, relative to the same qualities and abilities of other people.

Lake Wobegon Effect: A tendency to underestimate certain positive abilities and ignore defects. Also known by the bias name of optimism.

Self-Contention Bias: Tendency to distort cognitions to maintain self-esteem or keep your self-image extremely supportive.

Actor-observer bias: Also known as Correspondence Bias or Fundamental attribution error, it is the tendency to believe that what people do reflects who they are, regardless of situational and environmental factors involved in behavior.

Defensive attribution hypothesis: Assign more guilt to what harms someone as the outcome becomes more severe, or there is a greater similarity with the victim.

Personal Attribution Bias: Tendency to see yourself as less predictable than other people, directly relating your actions to your personality and not the environment and situation.

Justification by the effort: Tendency to give greater value to what it has put effort to realize.

Risk Compensation: Also known as the Peltzman Effect, a theory that suggests that people usually adjust their behavior in response to the perceived risk level, becoming more careful when they are at greater risk and less careful if they feel more protected.

2. To stay focused, we favor the immediate and the neighbor over the distant and backward. We value more of what is present to us in detriment of what is future, and we attach more to stories or individuals than to groups.

Hyperbolic discount: We give more value to immediate benefits than to future benefits. Just as we opt for immediate pleasures, we tend to procrastinate to the maximum. We can see this bias clearly when, for example, we leave our diet "for next week" that never arrives.

Appeal to novelty: A fallacy where it is proposed that something just because it is new is superior to what is old.

Identifiable victim effect: Refers to the tendency to respond more strongly to a single identified person at risk than to a large group of people at risk.

3. To conclude something, we are motivated to complete things in which we have already invested time and energy. This is the Behavioral Economy version of Newton's First Law. It is very likely that we will end activities that we begin with more than procrastinating for a while.

Cost-loss fallacy: Also known as the fall-back cost fallacy, it is a cognitive bias that causes the person who has had some injury to rationalize it and believe that it did the right thing.

Loss Aversion: It Is A Great Fear Of Losing That We Have

Irrational Escalation: Also known as Escalation of Commitment, it is a tendency for a person or a group of people to keep doing what has harmed them rather than changing behavior.

IKEA Effect: Also called Difficulty Processing Effect, the IKEA effect is a cognitive bias in which consumers attribute a disproportionately high value to the products they have partially created. The name derives from the name of the Swedish manufacturer and retailer of furniture IKEA, which sells many furniture products that require assembly.

Creation Effect: This effect tells us that information is more easily remembered when it is generated from one's own mind rather than read.

Zero risk bias: Tendency to prefer the complete elimination of a small risk to zero rather than to a large risk reduction.

Disposition Effect: This is an observed behavior in investors to sell shares with profit in a short period of time and hold shares at a loss for a long period of time.

Unit bias: Unit bias is the tendency of individuals wanting to complete a unit of a particular item or task. People want to finish whatever portion they have, no matter the size, it's a perception of completion that is satisfying to people.

Property effect: Effect Endowment, the tendency we have to value one more item because it is in our possession than if we did not have it.
Backfire Effect: When a person has his or her belief confronted by facts but instead of changing positioning increases their belief.

4. To avoid mistakes and irreversible decisions, we are motivated to preserve our autonomy and status in a group. If we need to choose, we will opt for what is less risky, or that preserves the status quo.

Reactivity (reactivation): It is an unpleasant motivational excitement (reaction) to offers, people, rules, or regulations that threaten or eliminate specific behavioral values.

Reverse psychology: A technique that involves the affirmation of a belief or behavior that is opposite to the desired, with the expectation that this approach encourages the subject of the persuasion to do what is really desired.

Asymmetric dominance effect: Asymmetric dominance effect's is the phenomenon by which consumers will tend to have a specific change in preference between two options when they also present a third option that is dominated asymmetrically.

Social Comparison bias: Having feelings of dislike and competitiveness with someone who is seen physically or mentally better than you.

5. We favor options that seem simple or have complete information about more complex or ambiguous options. We choose to perform simple and practical activities to the detriment of the most difficult and complex ones, even if the most laborious ones are a better energy expenditure.

Effect of ambiguity: Ambiguity effect is a cognitive bias in which decision making is affected by lack of information or "ambiguity." The effect implies that people tend to select options for which the probability of a favorable outcome is known, compared to an option for which the probability of a favorable outcome is unknown

Information bias: Tendency to look for information that will not actually affect decisions.

Belief bias: Belief bias is the tendency to judge the strength of the arguments based on the plausibility of their conclusion, rather than how strongly they hold this conclusion.

Effect of rhyme as a reason: Effect of rhyme as a reason is a cognitive bias with which a diction or aphorism is judged as more precise or true when it is rewritten to rhyme.

Effect of bike rack / Law of triviality: Effect of bicycle rack is an argument that members of an organization give disproportionate weight to trivial issues

Delmore Effect: The Delmore Effect, as defined by Paul Whitmore's doctoral dissertation (unable to find a good online copy), is our tendency to provide more articulate and explicit goals for areas of lower priority in our lives. It seems that the frightening nature of truly important goals can motivate the ego to deflect that anxiety by meeting less important but less threatening goals.

Conjunct fallacy: It is a formal fallacy that occurs when it is assumed that specific conditions are more likely than a single general.

Occam's Razor: The principle of problem-solving, which essentially states that "simpler solutions are more likely to be correct than complex ones."

Less effect is better: Effect less is better is a kind of inversion of preference that occurs when the minor or minor alternative of a proposition is preferred when evaluated separately, but not evaluated together.

Problem # 4 - What should we remember in all of this?

We are surrounded by information at all times. What exactly should we remember? We could not save as much information as we would like. We tend to prefer generalizations rather than specificities because they tell us a lot and take up little space. Details are important, but they are - alike - extremely costly to store.

1. Edit and reinforce some memories after the fact. Sometimes the memories can be sharper, but they are also highly editable. Often - unintentionally - we add false memories to our true memories.

Related Terms / Bias:

Error in memory allocation / Source confusion: Incorrect memory allocation refers to the ability to remember information correctly, but to be wrong about the source of this information.

Cryptomnesia: Occurs when a forgotten memory returns without being recognized as such by the subject, who believes that it is something new and original.

Confabulation: It is a memory error defined as the production of memories manufactured, distorted, or misinterpreted about oneself or the world without the conscious intention to deceive.

Suggestiveness: It is to be inclined to accept and act upon the suggestions of others where false but plausible information is given and fills the gaps in certain memories with false information when recalling a scenario or moment.

Spacing effect: It is the phenomenon by which learning is greatest when the study is distributed over time, rather than studying the same amount of content in a single session.
2. We discard specificities to form generalizations. We do not handle such complexity. The specificities that present us soon can be replaced by gross generalizations.

Related Terms / Bias:

Implicit stereotypes: It is the unconscious attribution of particular qualities to a member of a particular social group.

Prejudice: Prejudice is an affective feeling towards a person or group based solely on generalized characteristics of the group.

Bias of Negativity: The belief that even when of equal intensity, things of a more negative nature have a greater effect on the psychological state and processes than neutral or positive things.

Fading emotion bias: Fading emotion bias is a psychological phenomenon in which memories associated with negative emotions tend to be forgotten faster than those associated with positive emotions.

3. Reduce events and lists to their key elements. We chose to collect some items to represent a whole.

Related Terms / Bias:

Peak and end rule: It is a psychological heuristic in which people judge an experience largely based on how they felt at their peak (i.e., their peak) and at their end, instead of basing themselves on the sum total or average of each moment.

Leveling and grinding (molding): Sharpness is usually the way people remember small details in recounting stories they have experienced or are recounting those stories. Leveling is when people keep bits of stories and try to soften these stories so that some parts are deleted.

Disinformation effect: A disinformation effect occurs when the memory of episodic memories becomes less accurate because of post-event information.

Denial of Duration: The psychological observation that people's judgments about the dislike of painful experiences depend very little on the duration of these experiences.

Effect of sequence recall / Effect of list length: Serial recall is the ability to recall items or events in the order in which they occurred. The possibility of serial recall decreases as the duration of the list or sequence increases.

Effect of modality: Effect of modality refers to how the student's performance depends on the presentation mode of the items studied.

Memory inhibition: Memory inhibition is the ability to not remember information considered irrelevant.

Primacy Effect: It is easier to remember more of the positive words spoken at the beginning than the rest of the content.

Effect of recency / serial position: A tendency for a person to remember the first and last items of a series better, and to have greater difficulty in remembering the middle items.

4. We keep memories differently, relying on how we experience them. The way our experiences have occurred will predict how they will be remembered.

Related Terms / Bias:

Effect of processing levels: Effect of processing levels registers the memory of stimulus memory as a function of the depth of mental processing. Deeper levels of analysis produce more elaborate, longer-lasting, and stronger memory traits than the surface analysis levels.

Test effect: Test effect is the discovery that long-term memory is often increased when part of the learning period is dedicated to the recovery of the future.

Absent Mind: It is when a person demonstrates inattentive or forgetful behavior. It can have three different causes: a low level of attention ("blanking" or "zoning out"), intense attention to a single focus object (hyperfocus) that causes a person to be unaware of events around him or unwarranted distraction from object focus by irrelevant thoughts or environmental events.

Effect of the next line: Incomplete recall for an event immediately preceding an anticipated public performance.

"At the tip of the tongue" phenomenon: It is the phenomenon of not recovering a word from memory, combined with partial memory and the feeling that recovery is imminent.

Google Effect: Google Effect is the tendency to forget information that can be easily found online using Internet search engines such as Google.

Conclusion

Thank you for making it through to the end of *Mental Models*, let's hope it was informative and able to provide you with all of the tools you need to achieve your goals whatever they may be.

We are definitely not as rational as we think, we are biased at all times, but for a good cause:

Our survival!

Imagine if we had to use logic for everything, we would not endure such a day. It is true that these biases often get in the way of our choices, and therefore we must seek to understand more deeply our positions so that we do not make mistakes of judgments about ourselves and others. Note: Not all terms described above are behavioral biases recognized and supported by Behavioral Economics experiments.

To 'repeal' Murphy's law

We can eliminate Murphy's Law through substantial improvements in our planning and management process. A great amount of work is not delivered on time. Novelty? On the contrary, it is the rule. I would be surprised if it were delivered on time. An imported machine did not arrive on time. Surprise? Neither. This is a normal situation with uncertainties in ports and customs. The study for the launch of a new product was not ready in time to anticipate the product of the competition.

Unexpected? No, this had already happened in the previous release.

We have all gone through a similar situation where something did not go according to plan or expected. Something so recurrent leads companies to always get out of fires and create raids and generate stress.

In other words, the famous and ubiquitous "Murphy's Law" remains very current. The origins of this epigram, a concise phrase or concept loaded with irony and jocosity, are not clearly known. Some even call it a form of the second law of thermodynamics or law of entropy, which predicts a growing state of disorganization. In short, it says that "in any circumstance and situation, if something can go wrong, it will!"

Do we have to settle for it and consider it part of our personal or professional life? Not necessarily. We can eliminate Murphy's Law through substantial improvements in our planning and management process. What can we do to challenge and eliminate Murphy's Law? We can go on to elaborate more detailed and detailed plans, to always construct multiple alternatives and eliminate the idea of positive thinking.

We need, first of all, to work with more detailed and rigorous planning. Often, we define the actions to be carried out, forgetting many of them and not knowing in more depth what needs to be done. Thus, at the time of execution, many vacant items become difficult to deploy. The planning process is always more important than the plans themselves. Typically, conditions change and also require changes in plans. But the more rigorous, deeper, and more detailed the plan is, the easier our understanding and knowledge.

The second important dimension is always thinking and building multiple alternatives. This forces our mind to force the search for solutions other than what we think is right. In addition to helping to create concrete alternatives in case of necessary adjustments, a common fact due to changes in the context and conditions, it helps the mental process and the creativity, forcing the involved agents to be able to make the adjustments in the plans, increasing the flexibility and the speed of response.

And finally, the third dimension is to dispel positive thinking, the one that says "do not worry; everything will work out." Positive thinking or optimism can create a sense of relief and reassurance. But at the same time, it causes complacency and accommodation. Tranquility ends when unexpected problems arise.

Those who are not "optimists" are better prepared for adversity, because for them, as things can go wrong, they anticipate it. For those who use negative thinking that "anything can go wrong," the preparation and anticipation of problems stimulates the production of adrenaline and leaves people on alert.

It is not about creating depressive environments and people that generate a lack of action and immobility. Rather, it is about creating conditions for people and organizations to react in time and with the expected quality to the natural turbulence and uncertainties that will always occur. Preparing for the worst to happen is so much better than figuring that everything will go well. Of course, the character of law is a joke that scientists from the most diverse fields do. It is not even a question of nature or even the field of law.

Even so, Murphy's Law and its axioms will remain. It will not be possible to "revoke" it. And especially for those who plan poorly, without thinking about alternatives and without properly assessing risks and threats. Those who do differently, that is, plan accurately, establish alternatives, and anticipate adversities, will be able to mitigate their impacts.

The "Razor of Ockham" and the dissolution of traditional metaphysics

Born in the village of Ockham near London, approximately in the year 1280, Guilherme developed a methodological precept that had fruitful consequences for later philosophy. With this methodological character, Guilherme de Ockham gives place to a new scientific paradigm, denying all traditional metaphysics. Moreover, the separation of types of knowledge leads to a denial of all medieval tradition that was based on the union of philosophy and theology. Contrary to the Platonic metaphysics and the Platonic elements present in the philosophy of Aristotle formulated a statement defined as Razor of Ockham that says: "Do not multiply the beings if it is not necessary." This statement opens the way to a model of knowledge coming from the man himself, not requiring divine factors for it. With this, Guilherme sets up a methodology that later became known as the rejection of "ad hoc hypotheses."

Ockham's Razor consists basically of eliminating all possible excesses, thus creating a medieval (though not modern) science, which is obviously a prelude to modern physics. With the "Razor" a period ends, and another begins where the medieval paradigms are seen as inconsistent. Moreover, there is in Ockham's method a whole negation of Plato's and Aristotle's models. The platonic model that hierarchizes the universe into the intelligible world as a model for the sensitive world is left out. In the place enters a homogeneous universe in which things can be known by the empirical way. Clearly, multiplicity gives way to the homogeneity of beings in the face of an "economy" of reason, which tends to exclude from the world and science superfluous entities and concepts, beginning with metaphysical entities and concepts.

It can be seen that through Ockham not only in epistemology but also politics, is an aspiration for reform, which would become even more pronounced in the following century, culminating in the Protestant Reformation. With Ockham, scholasticism finds its apex, for, after him, no greater personalities or philosophical systems emerged. What happens is only the existence of scholars of Ockham, Aquinas, and Augustine, of Scotus, disputing their spaces for existing theories. Faced with these three other currents, Ockham emerges as a critic to the scholastic tradition, imposing a modern way, opposing the whole tradition of medieval thought. The influence and importance of Ockham, his "Razor" and consequently his scientific method preconize modern science. Philosophers of science claim the influence suffered by Galileo saying that "Galileo's genius consists in his use of the prospect possibilities made available by paradigm shifts in the Middle Ages."

Formulated by the medieval philosopher Guillaume de Occam (sometimes written Ockham), the lex parsimonious (law of parsimony) is a principle, problem solver, philosophical reductionist, which allows distinguishing between equivalent theories and can be used as a technique for the formulation of theoretical models. In its simplest formulation, Occam's Razor will say that between two theories with equal results, which explain or predict the same phenomena, we must always choose the simplest theory.

Occam's razor is often used to avoid unnecessary ontological inflations when an entity or substance is postulated, with no evidence of its existence simply to enable the application or consistency of a theory.

Before the twentieth century, the assumption that nature was simple, and thus, the simpler explanation would be more likely to be true. Thomas Aquinas argued in the thirteenth century that if something can be done by means of an element, it would be superfluous to do so through various elements, since nature employs only the necessary elements, never more than that. With the development of science, especially from the twentieth century, however, the idea that events may be more complex than our best theories suppose, and the defense of Occam's razor based on the assumption of the simplicity of nature, loses power.

In pragmatic terms, it is understood that simple theories are easier to understand. In this way, Occam's razor makes the presentation of theories simpler and the discussions more practical. Elliot Sober argued that strictly speaking, even reason itself cannot be rigorously justified and, in order to establish a promising dialogue, it is necessary to accept some elements beforehand. Occam's razor is, according to him, a good candidate to carry out the task to choose the elements from which the discussion will begin. Another justification for Occam's razor comes from mathematics, more specifically from the law of probability. It is understood that with each element introduced there is an increase in the possibility of errors. Thus, if an element does not increase the accuracy of a theory, its only effect is to increase the possibility that the theory is wrong.

The philosopher Karl Popper argued that our preference for simplicity could be justified by the criterion of falsifiability since a simpler theory would apply to a greater number of cases, it would be easier to test and falsify it than a more complex. On the other hand, Walter Chatton, a contemporary of Occam, considered Occam's behavior excessively minimalist and argued that if the entities or elements proposed are not sufficient to verify an affirmative proposition about something, other elements must be proposed until it can be verified. Among the philosophers who formulated anti-razors, we also find Gottfried Wilhelm Leibniz, Karl Menger, and Immanuel Kant. With variations of each author, the anti-razor position is generally a defense that the variety of beings should not be reduced precipitously, thus assigning a precipitous and extreme position to Occam.

Hanlon's Razor: Do Not Attribute To Evil What May Just Be Stupidity

Nowadays, people communicate more in writing than they speak (those with access to technology). His great-grandfather, for example, spoke more than he wrote. He would open the door to the house in the morning, go out into the street and spend the day talking to people. Today we also talk all day, but we do not even open our mouths.

Its zap-zap here, torpedo's there, email to work, Facebook to share, Instagram to show. All this because the writing has become more convenient than the speech. I rarely use the phone, only when it is a relative or friend, generally the situations in which you want to hear the voice of the person himself. Otherwise, it is annular artillery, and I leave submerged letters, click, click, and click.

But this transition from speech to writing is/was not so simple. As you may have noticed a long time ago, the spoken things work one way, and the written ones, another. When you are speaking, your speech has the intonation, the gesticulation, and a lot of clues that help the other person to understand you. In writing, despite the characteristic and the opportunity of more "thoughtful and elaborate" communication, these clues are not so easy to perceive. Other than that we're cutting it all down. And what does that mean?

The misunderstandings have increased. His chats are more subject to confusion than those of his great-grandfather. It's funny to realize that our communication potential has increased a bit, but so have the oxen on the line, those situations where you wanted to say one thing, but the person understood another. You write, "yesterday was great," and the person thinks "great? Only that? Humpf! ". You think you were nice and you think you were insensitive. We'll talk more. And less, too. If your great-grandfather's communication possibilities were "more or less," yours are "more and less." And that's why I think you should know and familiarize yourself with the concept behind Hanlon's Razor. I will try to explain this really quickly:

Philosophy, like the barbershop, has a lot of razors. But instead of shaving faces, the philosophical knives serve to cut the fat of hypotheses, which are the possibilities for explaining something. And .for that, Hanlon says the following:

It is the famous "benefit of the doubt." When in doubt, do not go finding the worst, or seeing badness right away. It may just be a case of naivety (or ignorance, or stupidity, etc.). When that dentist took the NEMO on the seabed and took it to the aquarium in his office, he was not a sucker. He did not even think about the implications; he even thought it would be good for the goldfish; it would be safer and well-fed. For Nemo's father, it was a kidnapping. In the end, it was the "ignorance" of the dentist, who turned out to be stupid (a word that sometimes confuses, but that means a mistake of the judgment of something).

In conclusion: From now on, every time you come face-to-face with something that leaves the doubt (and it will probably be in written form), remember Hanlon's razor and allow yourself the benefit of the doubt because it's usually an ox in the same line. This is especially important for those who give or receive WRITE commands and feedbacks. How often do you share an idea by email, and the reply is pure frustration or even criticism?

We managed to find the solution for mental models! After these 3 months of work, we finally killed the charade! It was fantastic, sensational and indeed, we are excited.

How Does the Pareto Principle Help Team Productivity?

When you have a team to lead, it is a challenging task. After all, you need to be a productive leader, and also train your team to be one. As we are in a time of transition from the traditional working models to new methods that take staff productivity into account - no longer the (long) hours worked inside the office, this is a fundamental task, and that should be put into practice as soon as possible in the corporate environment.

It is in this sense that the so-called Pareto Principle emerges as an important tool for changes in the way we work. The methodology was created more than 100 years ago and is more than necessary in such times when technology requires speed in the execution of tasks. In the following paragraphs, we will know better about this principle and how you can apply it in your day to day life and in the routine of your team. Keep on reading, people.

What Is The Pareto Principle?

Also known as Law 80/20, the Pareto Principle arose in 1906 and was formulated by Vilfredo Frederico Pareto, a Parisian with Italian nationality, who was an important engineer, sociologist, and economist of the time. But the principle was only disseminated in the 1940s, by Joseph Juran, a renowned specialist in quality management.

Pareto did not believe in the continuous effort, the one that you sacrifice at high levels to achieve some result. For him, the most important was productivity and its consequences for human life; that is, he believed that the effort had to be made only in what was really necessary to obtain a good result - the so-called selective effort.

While Pareto came to the conclusion that 20% of Italians owned 80% of the country's land, Juran furthered his studies and found that:

80% of the world's wealth is concentrated in the hands of 20% of the population.

80% of a company's revenue comes from 20% of customers.

80% of your personal satisfaction is the result of 20% of the people in your circle of friends.

20% of physical activity gives you 80% of the real benefits - and so on.

Therefore, it was concluded that this ratio 80/20 could be applied in all areas of life, both personal and professional and, over time, studies have shown that this proportion may vary, but the fact is that it's still worth it. So, when we refer to the world of work, how does the 80/20 Law apply? Simple:

20% OF YOUR EFFORT WILL BE 80% OF YOUR RESULT.

This is not to say that to get a good result; it is not necessary to work hard and hard, but rather to direct the efforts to the right actions that will produce those results. For this, you need to have a great degree of team productivity. You have to focus on what really matters; otherwise, there will be no goal attained (or it will be achieved under an uncommon effort and therefore will take longer).

Diagnosing Team Productivity Flaws With The Pareto Principle

Although simple, the process of applying the Pareto principle to the corporate routine is not instantaneous. After all, evaluating what the 20% effort that could represent the 80% improvement is not an easy task. It takes time and planning, but the results outweigh customer retention, cost reduction, waste elimination, increased sales, profitability, etc.

First and foremost, you need to stop and identify the shortcomings that are being made that prevent you and your team from being productive and delivering satisfactory results.

Two Important Tips:

1 Have a well-defined goal

Before you apply the Pareto principle in your company, you need to define the objectives for this application, such as:

- Waste disposal;
- The reduction/elimination of employee overtime;
- Reducing production costs;
- The increase in the customer retention index.

Notice that everything is linked, to a certain extent, to the performance of employees. Therefore, most efforts should be made to improve staff productivity.

How often are these errors? Which employees are responsible for these areas and where the failures occur? Based on this survey, the problems become clearer and why they occur, which helps with decision making and strategies to increase productivity.

Increasing Team Productivity

Here are some tips on how to increase team productivity by always observing the Pareto principle:

Learn to delegate tasks

First of all, you, as a team leader, need to apply the 80/20 Law in your own routine of work. For this, it is very important to decentralize tasks and learn how to delegate them.

Meaning? Knowing the weaknesses and strengths of your team to know what to expect from it and what tasks can be delegated to each. Be clear about the functions and what you expect, always charging the deadlines.

Teach your team to use the Prioritization Matrix

Although you have good collaborators, there may be a serious productivity problem. So it's time to train them to be better organized in their routines - and a good way out is the Prioritization Matrix. This technique helps - a lot - when it comes to defining what should be done with priority and what should not be done - especially if employees have a busy day.

The first step in adopting the prioritization matrix technique is to list everything that needs to be done, so it is so important that everyone have their agendas, whether virtual or traditional paper models. With the lists made, each employee should rank the tasks in more and less important, besides urgent or not. For example:

- Important is everything that, if done, will bring good results.
- Urgent is all that, if you do not, can bring trouble.
- Knowing this, tasks can be classified into an array in:
- Important and urgent: all that needs to be done now.
- Important and non-urgent: activities that, if they are not done, do not bring problems, but that, accomplished, improve something. That is, they are the ones that you decide when to do.
- Not important and urgent: if they are not done, they will not bring major problems. Usually, they are actions that can be delegated so that someone of confidence does them.
- Not important and not urgent: they are activities that you must forget because besides not bringing results, even if they are not done, they do not bring problems.

When we procrastinate, we usually perform these kinds of activities.

Establish Goals

Setting goals for the quarter and breaking them down into small tasks that can be easily managed and assigned is a great tip for measuring staff productivity. Also, do not forget to communicate to everyone the strategic vision behind every project, task, activity, etc. With well-informed staff, motivation and involvement grow.

Create an Environment That Promotes Efficiency

It is no use for the practitioner to want to apply the Pareto Principle to increase productivity and obtain more results if the work environment is not conducive to it. Imagine, for example, a graphic designer working on a practically obsolete computer, with little memory, old processor, and inadequate screen resolution? A store clerk who needs to register customers on paper chips, a market that does not have an automated stock control? Of course, it will be necessary to spend 80% of efforts to have the least results - the opposite of the 80/20 Law.

Reduce Unnecessary Tasks

Nothing is more disturbing than spending an entire day's work on unnecessary tasks that will not add value to the monthly result. It is as if an outside salesperson, for example, had to spend the whole day in the office cleaning some notes of his schedule. So be careful when asking your employees for tasks that are not urgent and important - if they do not contribute directly to the goal in question, reduce or eliminate it.

Beware of Meetings

Excessive meetings are great for procrastinating work and stealing time that could be used more productively. This is not to say that you should stop meeting with your team - on the contrary, this is important for the interaction and discussion of important points of the job. But be careful with the amount during the week, and also with the time spent to carry them out. If the focus here is 80/20, then, nothing is more certain than optimizing the time, is not it?

Reduce Reporting

Reducing red tape is also a great tip to increase team productivity and focus on what will really bring concrete results. If more than 10% of employees' day is spent producing reports about the work they are doing, there is something wrong. One way to address this reporting need is to automate processes to generate documents almost in real-time, and without wasting time.

Give Real-Time Feedback

Immediately recognize the positive actions of your team, and also address issues that need immediate improvement. Do not wait for a big day or a meeting to do this. Real-time performance feedbacks empower employees to take ownership of their work and build trust in process progress - which increases team productivity.

Take Away Distractions

How hard is that, isn't it? Emails come in every moment, messages from WhatsApp, and notifications from social networks, phone calls, etc. But if you want a productive company, you need to eliminate the distractions. This does not mean that, from today, your employees are prohibited from attending any personal phone call, for example. You need to encourage them to eliminate their distractions by applying the Prioritization Matrix.

Over time, of course, the positive results will appear, and the collaborators will not be drawn to excessive procrastination and lack of concentration. How about, in return, do you offer greater flexibility in working hours?

Invest in Internal Communication

One great tool to get rid of excessive meetings is to invest in effective internal communication. After all, a lot of information can be conveyed in this way, such as:

The Objectives ofthe Company

News about the market that can help in the work and the productivity of the team;

Important Announcements That Need To Reach Everyone

Important events and meetings that require the participation of all or a particular sector.

To do this, use internal channels such as newsletters, emails, newspapers, and even the bulletin board.

Just be careful with the periodicity of the posts, because in excess, can also generate a loss in the productivity of the team, which is bogged down with information and communications to be read and understood.

Provide Growth Opportunities to Employees

Team productivity is related to each member's knowledge, skills, and experience. Then, wherever possible, offer empowerment and training so that they grow and their talents are empowered. Your business makes a lot of money from this investment.

Invest In Adequate Food

Even the coffee time can be optimized within the company; by providing adequate food in the office environment, the need to exit employees is avoided. So invest in a resting and feeding space so that they recharge the energies with nutritious and balanced foods. If the budget is tight for this, encourage them to bring a snack or partner with a company in the industry.

Adopt a Reward System

Rewarding a collaborator for a goal is a great way to increase team productivity. In this case, the reward can be financial or in prizes of incentive simpler (like a pair of tickets for the long-awaited release in the cinema), for example, always stimulated the team to improve its performance.

As we have seen, applying the Pareto principle is a great way to focus on what will actually bring concrete results to the company and staff productivity. So, do not forget to deepen your knowledge in Management, including People Management, so that your company grow consistently, productively, and prepared for the market.

How to Make?

If you already have a company I suggest that you do this analysis through the Pareto Law and calculate which clients guarantee you 80% of the profits. You should focus your attention more on this segment, guaranteeing you more quality and personalized service. Do not say that you do not take an interest in the other 20%, but do not waste much time with them and if you have to lose some, do not worry. Focus on those who make a profit, and you will see your business grow.

If you are starting your business, the best is to (re) define your target audience and see which 20% can guarantee a large part of the revenue. With this analysis, you will save money and gain credibility, vis-à-vis the people involved in this niche market.

Time

After sharing with the readers what they should do to organize their day efficiently, the truth is that this law comes to support the part where I explain that should go against what is essential. If you analyze the time you lose from your day, you will see that in 20% of your activities you spend 80% of your time. It is true that there are times of the day that we cannot avoid, such as eating, sleeping, or bathing. However, if you want to improve productivity during your day, look at the other factors that cause the time to run out between your fingers.

- Does reading the e-mail about curiosities and at any time, is so important?
- To what extent do you part of WhatsApp groups that have little influence on mine is important?
- Does that Facebook game contribute to my goals?

Some people complain that they lack time and do not know how they will handle so many activities during the day. If you do this analysis, you will find that there are times of the day that your productivity tends to be zero. We may think that small distractions like the ones I mentioned above consume only part of our day, but the truth is that all of them, added to the end of the day, make the time available that seems much shorter.

How to make it? For a week, write down hourly what you are doing while you are working. In the end, look at the times you were producing and those you spent wasting time. The next week gets better by trying to lower the percentage of time lost to near zero.

Try to reduce that 20 % that consume much of your time. I know you can feel like a machine by pointing out what you are doing one hour at a time. But remember that this will be a temporary situation that only serves to confirm where you are actually investing your time and how to optimize to gain more time for relevant activities and even have plenty of time for you.

All behavior begins with analyzing the pattern of functioning, then assessing what changes are needed, what to do, how to do it and so on, until it becomes a habit, at which point the notation will no longer be important, it will be healthily automated.

You need to make sure that you are spending your time fulfilling the goals of the organization. There is no point working for an hour a day and then pretending to work for the remaining eight hours. It is important to be focused towards the end goal because this will have a twofold effect. As you put efforts towards the company's growth, your growth chart will also go higher. This is one of the benefits that is a result of hard work and determination.

You also need to understand how your team or your colleagues are working around you. There will always be that one employee that brings down the morale of the rest or tries to spread negativity. Apart from taking away distractions, keep away such people as well. As mentioned above, you need to reduce the things that consume too much of your time. If you feel that you are spending too much time with a colleague on a coffee break or trying to convince them to work, then you are wasting your time. Yes, you need everyone to be efficient but not at the cost of your own efficiency. These points need to be kept in mind in order to bring about consistency with work and growth for you and the organization.

Reading, Workshop and Courses

Wanting to learn is an essential attitude for anyone who wants to succeed in the current business, especially about the market that wants or is acting. Nowadays (and still well) there are thousands of options available on the internet for research and a wide range of books and ebooks that can be very useful for gaining knowledge, even for free. But how good is it to want to read about everything? This is a curiosity that only a few have; however, it is not that difficult to learn to adapt and become keen towards it.

What I mean is that sometimes we waste time reading or taking courses on certain subjects that will be of little interest to the development of your life, especially if time is scarce. Focus on what is related to your business area or that will generate value in your personal life.

How to Make?

If Pareto's law is correct in your case, you'll find that only 20% of everything you've done contributes to 80% of your knowledge in the area and to increase your well-being. Analyze what they are and focus on it in order to add value in your life in general.

Personal Finances

It is already known that expenses such as housing, car, or food contribute to much of the monthly expenses. What may make you shocked when you do the analysis is that these sources of expenditure often do not exceed 50%. If one of your goals is to save so that you can invest in your career or company, it is important that you analyze the superfluous expenses to guarantee you new resources.

How To Make?

For a month, point out the expenses you have every day. Take a look through the Pareto Law and see that 20% of the expenses are consuming 80% of your monthly expenses. Try to cut down on avoiding superfluous expenses that may be preventing you from opening your own business, making your dream trip, checking into your own home, changing your car, etc.

What Else Is Possible?

I know, just thinking about controlling and looking at what you have done of your time, money, choices, you can be lazy or think that the Pareto Law is merely fiction, but I will give you some advice here: do it now! I know that you may have difficulty accepting new things, having to train new behaviors or being afraid of what this analysis might reveal to you, but the truth is that sometimes we work overtime, we misuse our free time, and spend more than the bill. This is the time to understand that we end up sinning for details. The work expands to fill the time available for it.

CN Parkinson – The Parkinson's Law, or the Search for Progress (1957)

You've probably noticed that if you have ten minutes to write a report, you'll write it in ten minutes. But if you have four hours, it will take four hours to do the same. This is the essence of the "Parkinson's Law," unveiled for the first time in 1955 by the historian Cyril Parodying the typical socioeconomics essay, Parkinson "proved" his thesis by charting the growth of the British naval bureaucracy, at a time when its responsibilities were diminishing: more people were necessary to produce less than usual.

"It is the busiest man who has more free time than anyone else," Parkinson said people arrange work with time for themselves; what actually varies is not free time, but the efficiency. Highly interested in knowing how his law worked in the workplace, Parkinson sarcastically remarked that "an officer wants to multiply subordinates, not rivals" and those "officers get work for each other." Regardless of the actual amount of work, administrators continue to hire more subordinates simply because they want to appear more responsible and powerful, starting a chain reaction that requires more juniors and more supervisors without any appreciable increase in productivity. Despite the irony of Parkinson's, his law does work, both at work and at home. The busier you are, the more efficient you need to be. The emptier your day, the more time will be consumed to perform simple tasks. Considering human nature, endless tasks - like certain household cleaners - are a kind of gift from heaven.

How to Apply the Parkinson's Law

Parkinson noted carefully how the work is developed in the dependencies of the state. Based on his daily experience, he was able to discover patterns that allowed him to define his basic principles. Parkinson's Law can be summarized in three basic statements/rules:

"Work expands to fill the time which it has for its realization."

"The expenses increase until covering all the gains."

"The time devoted to any subject of the agenda is inversely proportional to its importance."

Since its inception, experts on the subject have proven several times the validity of the Parkinson's Law. It has also served as a guide to propose new methods of work and time management in the areas of productivity. The work expands to fill the time available for its accomplishment. This means that if you have an hour to perform a task, you will use one hour to do it. But if you have a month, it will take a month.

This principle is related to another statement that Parkinson called "The Law of Postponement." It states that when we have time, there will always be the tendency to postpone everything that needs to be done. But why does this happen? Simply because time is a highly subjective concept. It depends much more on our inner perception than on the actual passing of the hours.

Parkinson also noted that the more time we spend on a task, the more complex it becomes and the harder it is to complete it. If we have the feeling that for a long time ahead, we look more closely at the details and usually go around the edges, trying to cover even the smallest aspects of the task. However, if we have little time, we focus on doing the work without taking so many turns on the subject.

Parkinson also noted that the less important issues are those that end up occupying most of the time. This is why his third major statement, "The time spent on any agenda item is inversely proportional to its importance."

Although Parkinson's Law was defined after observing the bureaucracy, the truth is that it applies to virtually every person. And it not only implies aspects related to the administration of time but also extends to other areas of life, such as expenses or the organization of physical spaces. Parkinson points out that "Expenditures increase to cover all gains." This means that no matter how much you make, you will always find a way to "be on the edge" and even debt.

A person can live with a certain income without any problem. If your income increases, this does not mean that it will have a surplus going forward, but it will organize your finances so that it will not over anything. The result of all these standards of conduct is a great inefficiency. Time and money are never enough. However, if we look closely, this is due to the mistaken way in which we manage our activities. Interesting, right? And eye-opening!

Moving on to the next topic, let me ask you this: Do you know the benefits of a mental map? Do you have the practice of using it? If your answers were no, maybe it's time to reflect on the subject. After all, this is a tool that has helped many people in different areas, such as students, professionals, leaders, etc.

What Is A Mental Map?

Mental maps are diagrams that, through the systematization of the natural flow of the brain, help and make a total difference in the processes of learning, organization, and production. We can define this tool as a way of illustrating ideas in a way that relates them to each other, from a central thought, making them more tangible and concrete, and thus reaching objectives more easily.

At this point, it might have gotten a bit boring, but I urge you to continue reading and discover the benefits of the mind map. Keep going!

1. IMPROVE THE ORGANIZATION OF SEVERAL AREAS OF LIFE

You can, through this mechanism, order your daily activities and professional projects. By means of the map, you transform a long list of tasks or tasks to be memorized into something easy to understand, by putting one activity as the main one and associating others with it. With this, the development of any process is easily visible and, consequently, more organized.

2. AUXILIARY MEMORY ADVANCEMENT

This is a great way to memorize the required items. From the drawing up of the map, the person is forced to analyze each thought to design it in the best way, initiating the process of memorization. With the development of ideas, the memories are systematically organized in the brain through the images contained there, increasing memorization.

As we seek to increase our awareness of the diagram, we stimulate a broader view and come to understand everything more comprehensively, which further develops the arrangement of ideas and memorization.

3. BRINGS MORE QUALITY TO WORK

With the use of the maps, our perception is increased, and we get good results with the work done, be they personal, professional, or any other area. And with the enhancement of assimilation, decision making is more accurate and assertive.

Another benefit we can cite is the development of teamwork. Because with the easiest understanding of the ideas and division of tasks, the members of the group tend to have greater collaboration and understanding, which helps in the achievement of the objectives.

4. HELP IN THE DEVELOPMENT OF EMOTIONAL WELFARE

By bringing more organization, effective development, and better efficiency, this diagram reduces stress and increases self-esteem, resulting in emotional benefits as well. When we make use of this formidable tool, there is an interest in developing a certain activity, generating in us a greater sense of cooperation and control of the situation. In this way, we feel more confident and accept greater challenges without major problems.

5. PROMOTE THE ORGANIZATION OF ITS IDEAS BOTH IN PAPER AND IN COMPUTERIZED FORMATION

For some time now, making use of this tool was possible only through sheets of paper, but as the idea grew and more people became interested, the tool was computerized. So if you're the kind of person who prefers to use your computer or smartphone to get organized and work, you can rest easy, since there are a number of practical applications for creating maps today.

Benefits and Advantages of Mind Mapping

We usually do things for the benefits they provide to ourselves and/or others. Here's a list, divided into personal benefits, for groups and teams, and for a whole community. I suggest you read them after having a reasonable idea of what and how mental maps are. Check them out once:

Personal Benefits

1) Significant reduction of the physical volume of paper relative to notes and study material.

2) Significant reduction of the time of planning, elaboration, and revision of written tasks.

3) Significant reduction of the time required for planning, preparing, and preparing presentations.

4) Exceptional facility to restructure anything that has a structure.

5) Improvement of the quality of products with linguistic content in general, as they lead to good organization, coordination, and integration. For existing products, they evidence structure problems, such as in the sequence and intersections of content between parts.

6) In general, they increase productivity and competence.

7) Facilitate memorization and remembrance for being organized, containing images, and only essential ideas.

8) Develop the pursuit and perception of multiple aspects of a subject or situation.

9) Stimulate the vision of an idea in a broader context, rather than isolated, providing a more comprehensive and balanced understanding.

10) Develop objectivity, filtering ideas that do not fit the whole or that are not essential.

11) They develop the ability to organize knowledge, which is critical of how many of them we often have to deal with.

12) Facilitate the application of knowledge because it is a representation closer to that used mentally.

13) Provide an organized structure for the integration of the foreground.

14) Develop the skills of both synthesis and analysis, including structuring topics in categories.

15) They develop the ability to think through relationships, one of the bases of systemic thinking.

16) Stimulate freedom of thought and consequently, creativity, because brainstorming, or the free flow of ideas, is part of the mental map culture and provided by mind mapping programs.

17) They provide a structure for non-knowledge, that is, the structural parts of the map (variables) that do not yet have content, defining to the person precisely what he knows and what he does not know.

18) Reduce or eliminate the stress caused by excessive information and activities, and by their disorganization.

19) Because they are visual and colorful, they are more attractive and arouse more interest, particularly the younger ones, making them more receptive and cooperative.

20) Keeps the person in control of their creative and analytical processes and large amounts of information, with consequent greater predictability of results.

21) As a result, they generally expand the person's degree of security and tranquility, self-esteem, self-confidence, and a sense of capacity, with a consequent and natural acceptance of greater challenges.

22) Greater flexibility due to the broader and more complete view of a subject or situation and the perception of more alternatives.

23) Decisions become more precise and stable by considering more aspects and possibilities.

24) Facilitate group communication by giving a focus of agreement or divergence and placing all contributions in a context.

25) Training becomes more effective, either by the good structuring of the content, by the ease of study and revision, or by the better communication of the instructor.

26) Facilitate the coordination of the members through the better and easier division of tasks, within a global vision, increasing the probability that the goals of the group are reached.

27) Facilitate the sharing of knowledge by the distribution of mental maps.

28) The change in individual attitudes provided by long-term mental maps and systemic effects accelerated by the internet can significantly impact a whole country as a critical mass of people at home, in schools, and in businesses embody their capacities new ways of perceiving, thinking and deciding, driven and supported by this powerful tool.

The Human Potential Development Institute offers basic hands-on training on MENTAL MAPS in the Distance Education format intended for people who want resources to read and draw mind maps in a short period of time.

MENTAL MAPPING is a graphical method of information management that improves memory performance, contributes to the sharpening of reasoning and the development of intelligence. It is also excellent support for the creation of new knowledge and for increasing the focus of attention.

The accumulation of small problems, repeated daily, can have negative health consequences. You need to learn how to avoid stress.

Know some tips to combat the negative effects generated by excessive expectations, work, stress, and sadness. These tips will help you strengthen your mental health, and it will help you make sound decisions.

- Work with reality. At this point, it is important to make a self-assessment, but it is necessary to adapt the expectations generated at the beginning of the year with the reality that unfolded throughout it. The results of this self-assessment should take into account the possibilities that have been achieved to reach the goals and objectives sought.

- Be close to people who do you good. It may seem like obvious advice, but in this period, it is critical to choose to be alongside people who love us, who do good, who care about us. Support from family and friends is a protective factor against suffering.

- Take care of your body. The end of the year also brings an increase in the number of parties and parties, which can be a full plate for food cravings! Be modest, feed yourself well and without exaggerations of sweets or alcohol. In addition, it is important to maintain a physical exercise frequency of at least three times a week. It has been scientifically proven that combining a balanced diet with physical activities is a factor that helps to combat physical and mental illnesses.

One of the professionals who attended Tatiana said that she was stressed, but not the way people are conditioned to deal with the case - which is more related to day-to-day tiredness. Stress does not appear in any category in the international classification of diseases, but its effects are observed in the offices of the most diverse medical specialties such as cardiologists, endocrinologists, and psychiatrists.

The accumulation of small problems, repeated every day, can have consequences like increased blood pressure and the number of heartbeats that undoubtedly have negative consequences for the body.

Some of these changes are reflected in the body in the form of compulsions, anxiety, hair loss, skin problems, digestive tract malfunction, poor sleep regulation, weight gain or weight loss, menstrual cycle imbalance, and depression. This last point can be considered one of the most serious.

The festive mood at the end of the year brings with it an expectation that all people are in the same tune, but some are going through a stressful time, with big worries and suffering, and cannot match that moment. There are even studies that show that at very significant dates with a great emotional load, such as those at the end of the year, there may also be an increase in the incidence of suicides. You need to be aware of your family's and your loved ones mental health. It is never too late, and you need to make sure that you are in control of everything. I hope this book has helped you understand what mental health is all about and how you can make the most of your thought processes.

Finally, if you found this book useful in anyway, a review on Amazon is always appreciated!

www.ingramcontent.com/pod-product-compliance
Lightning Source LLC
Chambersburg PA
CBHW070706250726
48662CB00001B/279